THE WAR AGAINST HOPE

THE WAR AGAINST HOPE

HOW TEACHERS' UNIONS HURT CHILDREN, HINDER TEACHERS, AND ENDANGER PUBLIC EDUCATION

ROD PAIGE

Published by
THOMAS NELSON
Since 1798

www.thomasnelson.com

Published in Nashville, Tennessee, by Thomas Nelson, Inc.

Thomas Nelson, Inc. titles may be purchased in bulk for educational, business, fund-raising, or sales promotional use. For information, please e-mail SpecialMarkets@thomasnelson.com.

Library of Congress Cataloging-in-Publication data

Paige, Rod.
 The war against hope : how teachers' unions hurt children, hinder teachers, and endanger public education / Rod Paige.
  p. cm.
 Includes bibliographical references and index.
 ISBN-10: 1-59555-002-X
 ISBN-13: 978-1-59555-002-6
 1. Teachers' unions—United States. 2. Educational change—United States. I. Title.
LB2844.53.U6P34 2007
331.88'11371100973—dc22

2006039112

Printed in the United States of America
07 08 09 10 QW 5 4 3 2 1

I dedicate this book to all of the children
in this country whose education
has been compromised over the years
by the actions of teachers' unions
acting in their own self interest rather than
the best interests of their students.

It's time to admit that public education operates like a planned economy, a bureaucratic system in which everybody's role is spelled out in advance and there are few incentives for innovation and productivity. It's no surprise that our school system doesn't improve: It more resembles the communist economy than our own market economy.

—ALBERT SHANKER
Former President, American Federation of Teachers[1]

CONTENTS

PREFACE

THE ELEPHANT IN THE ROOM

An overflow crowd packed the grand ballroom of Washington DC's Renaissance Hotel for the opening plenary session of the 17th Annual Milken Family Foundation's National Education Conference. Foundation chairman Lowell Milken kicked off the conference with a fiery keynote address calling the audience's attention to America's education challenges and admonishing the crowd about the national need for new developments in teacher education.

The place was filled with excitement when Mr. Milken finished his remarks. Having brought his address to a potent ending, he bowed several times to the appreciative audience and then turned to introduce us, the five panelists who were up next to discuss "The Role of the Private Sector in Enhancing Teacher Quality." Like an announcer presenting the contestants in a championship sporting event, Mr. Milken proudly introduced "the members of our outstanding panel":

- Mr. Sandy Kress, Partner, Akin Gump Strauss Hauer and Field, LLP;
- Mr. Richard Lee Colvin, Director, Hechinger Institute on Education and the Media;

- Ms. Russlyn Ali, Executive Director, The Education Trust-West;
- Mr. Dan Katzir, Managing Director, The Broad Foundation; and
- Dr. Rod Paige, Senior Advisor, Higher Ed. Holdings, LLC; and Chairman, Chartwell Education Group LLC.

"This is a heavy-duty group," I thought to myself. And I was right: the panelists were outstanding. Inspired by their passionate presentations, the audience joined in for a spirited question-and-answer session. The group—made up of educators from across the nation, the Milken Teachers of the Year winners, education researchers, education journalists, business leaders, and others—posed a variety of questions. They asked about strategies to improve teacher quality, the effects of school culture, issues related to teacher compensation, the role of parents, and other such topics.

After about forty minutes of lively discussion, Mr. Milken instructed, "There is time for only one more question." Pointing to the back of the room, he decreed, "Last question, the lady in the back."

I noticed a distinguished-looking woman reaching for the mike. Turning to face the stage, she said in a confident voice:

I am [Jeanne Allen] from the Center for Education Reform. You've all provided an incredible amount of depth and breadth to both the problems and the solutions, and I commend you for doing it really comprehensively. But with all due respect, Lowell, there's an elephant in the room that hasn't been mentioned.

Before the 1960s, there were associations that supported, defended, and held to high expectations educators all across the country. Somewhere in the 1960s there was a transition where those associations stopped coming to the fore and actually became professional unions. Now they're just unions, not even professional, as some would argue.

What happened? Where is that in the discussion? Most people don't really comprehend and think about some of those root causes.

Are they causes? Are they problems we need to think about? Does the public need to know about it? What happened in that transition that we can learn from?[1]

The audience seemed stunned. For a moment, it was so quiet you could have heard a pin drop. Then, almost in unison, the people in the room turned their attention to the stage to see which of the panelists was going to tackle the question. The other panelists, two on either side of me, were staring at me. On the spot, I snapped, "Why is everyone looking at me?" One of the panelists answered, "You know why."

Yes, I did know why. But the more important "why" question was still on the table, untouched and unanswered. Why hadn't this group of esteemed scholars talked about the elephant in the room? Jeanne Allen's words were still echoing in my ears.

The behavior of the big, all-powerful teachers' unions is unquestionably the most significant determinant of the success or failure of most education reform efforts. But we had just spent two hours discussing education reform without even mentioning them. That in itself is a major statement about where we are in terms of improving America's system of education.

Why don't we talk more openly about teachers' unions and their influence? Why do we avoid speaking honestly about what they do (or don't do) to influence school reform efforts, and what they need to do differently? One possible explanation is that we have come to accept their actions against reform as inevitable—as a fact of life. But another logical reason for this absence of discussion is that the nation isn't fully aware of the destructive impact that many teachers' unions are having on the education of America's children.

The conversation that day made me realize more than ever just how urgently this book is needed, and I redoubled my efforts to finish writing it. I wanted to shine a bright light on teachers' union behavior and increase the probability that, in conferences such as the one I just described, we can begin to openly discuss and debate the influence of these massive organizations and consider how they must change in order to support and spur reform in our public education system.

THE URGENT NEED FOR CHANGE

Since 1965, Americans have spent hundreds of billions of dollars, millions of hours, and an immense amount of political capital trying to improve our underperforming public school system. Charles M. Payne sums up the payoff for this gargantuan effort in a sermonizing paper entitled "So Much Reform, So Little Change."[2]

Why are the results so limited? There are multiple reasons, of course. But the biggest one is that America has yet to muster the courage, and the political will, to confront the major barrier to authentic public education system reform: the National Education Association (NEA) and other self-aggrandizing teachers' unions. Until we as a nation face up to their systematic efforts to thwart meaningful change, all the billions of dollars, millions of man hours, and immense political capital spent on public education reform will be—to borrow from Shakespeare— "but a tale told by an idiot, full of sound and fury, signifying nothing."[3]

To "fix" our public education system, we have to significantly change the way schools and school systems currently operate. This requires changes in behavior for school boards, superintendents, school administrators, teachers, and parents—everyone involved in the education enterprise. This means that teachers' unions, too, must change. Some local affiliates have, in fact, done so. Recognizing the urgency of change and their shared responsibility for making it happen, these groups have decided to be productive partners in the fight for reform. But sadly, they are the exception rather than the rule. And their national leadership remains tenaciously insistent on preserving and protecting the status quo.

The problem is, big teachers' unions like the NEA don't want the current system to change. In fact, they are deeply threatened by the idea. Why? Because the status quo is working extraordinarily well for them. They experience no consequences for school failure, and they have no incentive to improve student performance. Their major goal is to collect union dues. They don't collect more union dues if student achievement improves. They may even be better off if student achievement does not improve, because such an environment creates the kinds of tensions that cause more teachers to seek the protection of the union's legal assets. In many states, teachers are forced to pay union dues whether they want to or not. So, why should the unions change?

Given this reality, it's quite unproductive to sit around idly, being upset with the aggressive, outrageous actions of many teachers' union leaders, hoping they will, out of the goodness of their hearts, change. They will not. They are simply doing their job, taking care of their organizational goals. Admittedly, their tactics often extend beyond the boundaries of decency, but nonetheless, they are still doing their job: taking care of their own interests.

The problem is not their behavior but our behavior: the public's behavior, us. While they are doing their job, taking care of their needs, we—the public—are not doing our job, taking care of the children's interests. Our inaction, standing by and putting up with excessive union intrusion in school operations, provides fertile ground for their resistance to reform. Thus, the public is both the villain and the victim in this story.

The tragic thing is that our unchallenged acceptance of excessive union intrusion in school operations is a strong accelerant of school failure. In fact, I would go so far as to say that the decline in our education system over the past several decades parallels the rise in influence of teachers' unions.

It is remarkable to me that, even in the face of massive student underperformance and failure, we, the public, passively take in stride teachers' unions' explanations for the deplorable performance of our education system. We are all too willing to accept, without careful scrutiny, their proposed solutions to the problems in our schools and sit back comfortably while they turn a system intended to advance children into a system operated to assure employment sanctity for adults.

Lest the reader be left with the wrong conclusion, let's stop now and make a few things clear. My concern here is not with the existence of teachers' unions, or unions in general. History provides many examples of situations where union support was appropriate, essential, and sometimes even noble. An excellent example is the virtuous work of a union called the Brotherhood of Sleeping Car Porters. During the 1920s, '30s, and '40s, it rescued thousands of black men who were serving as sleeping car porters from the inhumane working conditions imposed by the Pullman Company.[4]

Teachers too, unfortunately, are sometimes subjected to conditions that require the assistance of appropriate union support. It's a sad reality of our noble profession. Furthermore, some of what the teachers' unions have achieved historically has been not just productive, but at times even praiseworthy. No, my concern is not with unions per se, but rather with their leaders' behavior in blocking meaningful and urgently needed change. I firmly believe that teachers' union activity has gone well beyond the boundaries of appropriateness and far into the realm of excessiveness. This book is filled with examples.

How do they get away with this, one may ask? First, teachers' unions are extremely skillful at hiding behind America's love for teachers. They carefully refer to themselves as "the teachers," being vigilant never to classify themselves as "the union." Even in union contracts, they cautiously often avoid the term *union*, preferring most times to use a more benign term such as *the association*.

Admittedly, teachers' union members are teachers. But there is a major difference between the term *teacher* and the term *union*. A teacher is an individual—a person with unique views, aspirations, qualities. The union is an organization, an association, an establishment to which many, many teachers belong. Teachers have interests. Likewise, organizations and associations have interests. Ideally, the organization or association and its members have the same interests. But there are situations where the organization or association and their members may have widely different interests, and widely different views.

The union establishment is also very careful to use rhetoric designed to convince an unquestioning public that they act on behalf of children. But the reality is that unions exist to advocate on behalf of the unions' interests, not the children's.

This does not mean that teachers' unions don't care about the children. Of course, their individual members do (the vast majority of them, anyway). But teachers' unions taken as a whole almost never put children's interests ahead of the interests of the union establishment. First and foremost, their primary goal is to strengthen the union as an organization and to protect and enhance their constituents' well-being. That's their purpose. That's what they do. That's why they do as they do, and it would be quite naïve to expect them to do otherwise. Behavior is goal directed—this is a psychological truism.[5] To understand their goal is to understand their behavior.

Consider the following statement that appeared in a bulletin from the Oregon Education Association, a NEA affiliate: "The major purpose of our association is not education, rather it ought to be the extension and/or preservation of our members' rights. We earnestly care about kids and learning, but that is secondary to other goals."[6] I rest my case.

Throughout this book, I present examples of the ways in which teachers' unions' actions reveal their real purpose, which is to enhance the power of the union establishment. In analyzing these examples, I consider the many ways in which this purpose directly conflicts with and undermines the goals and purposes of school reform that are underway in schools and school districts across the country.

So, this book is not about bashing teachers' unions. It's about explaining them. To return to the metaphor that Ms. Allen introduced, it's about seeing the elephant for what it is and characterizing how it behaves. It's about making the teachers' unions' goals and actions more transparent, so that we—the public—can know them better and understand what they are doing more clearly. By providing information about teachers' unions, my hope is that we, the public, will decide to pay more attention to their activity in our schools, and rise up and challenge them when their actions threaten to keep our children from getting the education they deserve.

1

THE FIRESTORM

I t began as just another quiet meeting at the White House on a cold, gray day in late February 2004. Inside, the National Governors Association (NGA) had convened to hear about a variety of issues from President Bush's cabinet officers. The NGA, typically a bipartisan, strictly nuts-and-bolts affair, mostly focused on issues of the state and federal relationship.

When the members of the NGA get together, they represent some of the best minds and boldest reformers in America. James Madison called the states "laboratories of democracy"[1]—places where new ideas could be launched and the voice of the people could be heard. And so it was an honor for me to address this group. Many of the most promising ideas in education were the result of hard work by the men and women seated in that White House dining room.

As secretary of education, I spoke about all the promising reforms underway in education, at both the national and state levels. But at the same time, I could not help but reflect on my increasing frustration. Here were men and women who could understand the challenges that come with trying to change America's education system. They clearly understood the need for accountability in public education, and for linking funding to results. They clearly understood the thinking behind the No Child Left Behind Act (NCLB), a bipartisan law signed less than two years prior by President George W. Bush, joined by top leaders from both parties.

The problem was that the message about increased spending and new accountability wasn't getting through. While education spending continued to go up year after year, millions of Americans were being told that the federal government was spending *less,* not more, on our schools. Everyone in the world of politics and education knew who was promulgating that erroneous message. Everyone knew that this organization had not changed its message for nearly forty years. The force behind the partisan political attacks on No Child Left Behind was the National Education Association. Standing there in the nation's capitol, I could not help but think of the utterly destructive influence of the NEA and its lobbyists. Students, teachers, parents, and the public at large had so much to gain from the No Child Left Behind Act. But that did not matter.

It was then, in a moment of frustration, that I likened the NEA to a "terrorist organization" for its opposition and smash-mouth tactics that were holding the futures of millions of kids hostage.

The words had barely escaped my lips when I realized just how foolish and inappropriate the remark was. I had meant it as a grim joke, to describe the fear and scare tactics being used to obfuscate the issues and obstruct real reform. But I immediately wished I had not chosen such inflammatory language.

A silence came over the room. Even so, I continued with my remarks, but when I walked away from the speaker's podium, I knew that nothing else I said would be heard. The remark would get out. No one would consult me for clarification, context, or intention. This was Washington.

In the Bible, in the book of Ecclesiastes, is the warning: "Many have fallen by the edge of the sword; but not so many as have fallen by the tongue." I knew that the consequences were yet to come. It didn't take long. Soon the story was coursing along the wires and cable news programs.

I am not a creature of Washington. I came to the city to get things done, not to pad a résumé or aspire to a higher office. I was angry at myself because I had seen enough in my three years as secretary of education to know that this kind of impetuous linguistic mistake was just what my opponents wanted. As a former football coach, I knew that this was the article in the paper that the opposing coach would cut out and pin to the bulletin board to motivate his team into a fighting fury.

But the volatile reaction to my inadvertent and poor choice of words showed exactly what is wrong with our nation's public debate about education. In one single phrase, I garnered more attention than most editorial boards had given to the needs of children in a month of coverage. The editorial responses and opinion pieces in the nation's newspapers published every myth about public education, spread every message of fear, and told every story of woe that had slowed the reform initiative of No Child Left Behind and had frozen education reform long before President Bush had come to office in 2001.

The attacks on my comments fell roughly into three groups: those who objected to brutal language in politics; those who maintained that it was an attack on teachers because teachers and teachers' unions are the same; and those who viewed the remark as a sign of an administration that would brook no opposition and was imposing unfair requirements on America's education system.

The first group of critics, I could understand—good-hearted people who regretted the harsh tone of Washington politics. (I am in that group. When I apologized, I made that clear in my first paragraph.) The editorial board of the *Hartford Courant* said it was "bad politics, bad manners and just plain wrong," adding that my words were "reckless remarks."[2]

The *Houston Chronicle* stated, "There's no denying Paige's passionate support for Bush's education agenda, but opposing the president's policy is no act of terrorism—except maybe in a dictatorship."[3] An interesting phrase, because this was exactly what I was fighting against: a system that imposed its will on parents and children and gave citizens little choice in how their children were going to be educated. The *Chronicle* added, "By maligning the NEA with an inflammatory label, Paige strengthened his critics' hand and weakened the administration's."[4] Unfortunately, that was all too true.

The second group of critics was the political activist corps, those special interests who try to convince the public and teachers that teachers' unions are the same as teachers. They impugn the motives of anyone who questions the impact of teachers' unions, demands real academic results for children, or supports choice for parents. Their most potent weapon is their exploitation of America's honest love and admiration for outstanding, hardworking teachers.

Democratic National Committee Chairman Terry McAuliffe took this tack, saying that "[calling the National Education Association a 'terrorist organization' is] the most vile and disgusting form of hate speech—comparing those who teach America's children to terrorists."[5]

Pamela Johnson Taverner said her reactions ranged from "incredulous to stunned to shocked to appalled to furious, to, ultimately, sick at heart." Taverner added, "There is no distinction between the NEA and its members. We are the NEA." It is not surprising Taverner is so insistent on this point. She served on the NEA's national board of directors for the previous three years.[6]

The NEA's well-paid political leadership goes to extraordinary lengths to defend the myth that they are one with the nation's teaching corps. Nothing would threaten the NEA and the American Federation of Teachers (AFT) power politics more than the revelation that they are out of touch and out of sync with those they claim to lead. In the *Record*, of Bergen County, New Jersey, a recently retired "NEA activist," stated, "I have attended many annual NEA assemblies along with more than 9,000 other representatives from the United States and abroad. We assemble annually to do the business of the association and do what is good for public school children. Our members and our association are one and the same. The two can't be separated."[7]

The third group used the remarks to attack No Child Left Behind and the Bush administration under the guise of caring about the education debate. For the most part, these tended to be the very organs of opinion that were perpetuating the false claims that No Child Left Behind was underfunded. The *St. Louis Post-Dispatch* represented the view of this group. Calling my remarks "way out of line," they claimed that the president had failed to fully fund the law. As their editorialists put it, "The president had authority to seek $32 billion for education in the current fiscal year but requested less than $23 billion. Congress ended up providing about $25 billion."[8] This issue of spending was a red herring in discussions about real reform, given the record spending that accompanied NCLB. In addition, this argument bought into the bait-and-switch tactics of Washington spenders. They routinely promised more thorough "authorizations," which represent the *upper*-limit of spending, not the bare minimum or a reasonable amount as requested by the president.

Like many critics, the editorial writers at the *St. Louis Post-Dispatch* also sounded a defeatist note about education reform: "Another sore spot [in the law] is the requirement that schools bring all children up to proficiency by 2014 and make a certain level of progress each year. Many educators say this is unrealistic."[9] Is it unrealistic to want students to be able to achieve on grade level? If it is unrealistic, then why spend the money at all? If the schools can't do the job because the children can't learn, then why be concerned about their future? Ultimately, this was the real challenge in my job: to focus attention on students, not on spending—and to raise our expectations.

But while plenty of people were outraged by my careless wording in the wake of 9/11, many more were supportive of my intent. "Of course Rod Paige was wrong when he called America's most powerful teacher's union a 'terrorist organization.' Al Qaeda isn't nearly as bad at terrorism as the NEA is at educating our children," quipped columnist Michael Graham.[10] After noting the high cost of education and low levels of student achievement, Graham concluded even more acerbically: "Calling the current school bureaucrats 'terrorists' would actually extend them the compliment of assuming they are doing such a lousy job on purpose."[11]

Others were more serious, urging that the incident not distract anyone from the real issues at hand. Dacia Toll, director of the Amistad Academy, wrote, "While I do not defend [Paige's] cavalier remark, I hope that his apology means we will move quickly past this issue and focus our collective energies on the urgent task ahead. . . . In America today, black and Latino students by 12th grade lag more than four years behind their white peers. Secretary Paige is a life-long educator who has made it his mission to close this achievement gap."[12]

And as the editors of the *Virginian-Pilot* pointed out, "[No Child Left Behind] is controversial because it no longer allows school systems to mask the failures of disadvantaged children in the higher overall averages of the entire student body."[13]

What is amazing is that so few of the dozens upon dozens of articles criticizing my unfortunate quip alluded to the real problems: the abysmal scores, achievement gaps, and the mediocre achievement of America's schools as a pressing reason to drive reform.

I wanted nothing more than to return the nation's attention to those real issues, but first I had to figure out how to get past this controversy. It was a difficult time.

On Day Three of the firestorm, there was one moment of levity, however. My executive team meeting at the Department of Education had just ended, and as I sat down at my desk to finish reading the news clips for that morning, my secretary's voice came over the intercom system.

"Mr. Secretary, Secretary Powell is on Line One for you," she said.

"Colin Powell?" I inquired.

"Yes," she responded, "Secretary Colin Powell."

Colin Powell is one of the nicest, smartest, friendliest human beings one could ever meet. He is also known to seldom miss an opportunity to crack a joke. I remember wondering what he could want. In fact, his call gave me enough pause to make me contemplate how I should answer the phone. I decided on a formal approach.

"Good morning, Mr. Secretary," I said in a strong voice.

"Good morning, Rod. Cut the formal crap. I've got a deal for you," he said, just as strong.

"Really?" I asked. "What is it?"

"You do education, and let me do terrorism," he quipped, breaking into a hearty laugh.

For the next thirty seconds or so, we were both cracking up on our respective sides.

When the laughing died down, I said, "Colin, I've got a better deal for you."

"What?" he inquired.

I responded, "I'll take Arafat, and you take the NEA."

Without hesitation, he said, "Do I look like I am nuts?"

We both burst into laughter again.

And that's the way it was with many of my fellow cabinet members, many members of Congress, friends, and well-wishers from across the nation. They called, sent e-mails, wrote letters, all with supportive messages like "Keep your head up" and "It's just the way the system works."

So, even as the heat increased, friends and supporters circled the wagons. Furthermore, I had become accustomed to being under fire. For nearly three years, I had watched as critics and pessimists, naysayers and carpers, grumbled on the sidelines of the education debate, waiting for a mistake or a weakness to exploit. Many were mouthing nominal support for education reform and the importance of focusing on children rather than on the system. But all the while, they were looking for ways to turn personal attacks on the president, his cabinet, and his supporters into the death knell for reform.

Such is life inside the Washington Beltway.

In the world of power politics, US-style, nothing works better for special interests than to level *ad hominem* attacks on reformers. The reason is simple: Personal attacks attract media attention by adding to the drama and heightening the stakes in the horserace. Personal attacks distract from the real issues so that antireformers can deflect scrutiny. And they obscure the case being made by reformers when the critics and carpers are trying to defend their own power and interests.

It happened to Ronald Reagan when he sought to cut taxes; he was attacked as a doddering old man and a heartless enemy of the poor. It happened to Newt Gingrich when he had the courage to talk about the deep problems threatening Medicare, exposing the abysmal bureaucratic waste of Health Care Financing Administration and advocating the need for deep, meaningful reform for the sake of the elderly. Gingrich was accused of supporting "savage" and "draconian" cuts in the social safety net.

After three years working within the administration, I saw this personal attack gambit used regularly against President George W. Bush whenever he sought reforms to make government accountable to citizens—especially when it meant real accountability for how educators served children and parents. The strategy was not one-sided, of course; personal attacks had also been used regularly by Republicans during the Clinton years.

I had not come to Washington to join the race for power in the nation's capitol. At my age, with my commitment to principle and my proximity to retirement, I did not share the DC obsession with the next step—a higher office, cashing in, etc. I wanted to bring positive reform to our nation's schools, close the achievement gap between the races, and raise expectations for every child and every school. Nothing more, and nothing less.

Because this was Washington, I knew I had to do something to bring this controversy to a close. With my raw phrase being exploited by opponents of reform, the very real danger was that we would go back to the bitter partisan politics of the past—the politics that had prevented real reform for decades. I decided to fight. But first I had to convince the White House it was the right thing to do. President George W. Bush had come to Washington seeking to "change the tone in Washington," a promise that was real to every member of his team. Trying to go on offense was difficult and required me to meet with key White House communications personnel in order to get into the public arena to directly rebut the mounting criticism.

First, I penned an article for the *Washington Post* to apologize for the remarks. I wrote:

Education should be about children, not partisan politics. Yet, sadly, there has been a lot of political posturing on this issue lately. It may be inevitable during an election year. I admit that this week I, too, ratcheted up the debate with a very poor word choice to describe the leadership of the nation's largest teachers union. I chose my words carelessly, and I am truly sorry for the hurt and confusion they caused.[14]

I then used the rest of the article to set the record straight.

The principal critics of [NCLB]—aside from those with issues concerning federalism—fall into three camps: protectors of the education establishment, such as the national union lobbyists; some state legislators, who have become victims of an organized misinformation campaign; and, perhaps most sadly, some members of Congress who voted for the law and support its ideals but now see opposition as being to their political advantage. These forces have nothing to offer in place of the No Child Left Behind Act but demands for more money to pay for the same programs that haven't worked in the past.[15]

Money is the easy answer in politics. In three out of four cases, you know politicians are not serious about solving a problem when they simply think that more money will do the job. In education, especially, money is an easy way out. Because so many special interests are feeding off different parts of the education system, the only way to preserve balance in the status quo is to ask for more. To reform anything in education would threaten the power base of some part of the coalition of groups defending the status quo.

The education system has become like so many monopolies. Special interests have not only grown up and attached themselves to the status quo; in fact, they also go to extraordinary lengths to defend and preserve the status quo because they profit so handsomely from the privilege, power, and political influence that it provides them. Teachers' unions are especially resistant to any reform that threatens to break up their monopoly, provide options through deregulation and innovation, or put power in the hands of parents to demand accountability and choices in the school system. All of these issues are precisely what No Child Left Behind was designed to address.

NCLB demands accountability, which is exactly what the public needs. The education bureaucrats fear accountability because it lays bare what is not working. But nobody wants to come out and say they are opposed to greater accountability. So the critics' only recourse, in trying to destroy this seminal law, is to resort to the spending issue, trying to argue that not enough is being spent to enact worthwhile reforms. The money issue is a tempting escape route for the political and educational elite because it distracts from real debates about real reform. Increased spending raises the issues of deficits and taxes so that the old debates about those issues further cloud the discussion about how schools are serving (or not serving) children and parents.

That is why, in my response to the furor I had created, I focused on the needs of children and the urgent task of improving schools. For instance:

> The Nation's Report Card (the National Assessment of Educational Progress, or NAEP) shows that only one in six African Americans and one in five Hispanics are proficient in reading by the time they are seniors. NAEP math scores are even worse: Only 3 percent of blacks and 4 percent of Hispanics are testing at the "proficient" level. No wonder a recent study claimed a high school diploma has become nothing more than a "certificate of attendance."[16]

Facts like this make one thing perfectly clear to me: America's schools simply must improve, or else every hope we have of sustaining our great democracy and our vibrant economy is lost. As former Federal Reserve chairman Alan Greenspan once said, "We need to be forward-looking in order to adapt our education system to the evolving needs of the economy and the realities of our changing society."[17] Reforming the schools is an effort of the greatest urgency.

The big question is, *can* the system improve? I believe it can, and it will. However, what is clear from my decades-long experience with American education—from my time as a teacher in the small, intimate setting of the classroom to my position as United States secretary of education, meeting a room full of the nation's governors—is that while the status quo cannot stand, its defenders are willing to bear any cost and hold hostage every child's future to preserve it and defeat change. The chief defenders of that status quo are the National Education Association and the American Federation of Teachers, and as long as we see them as one with teachers, we are not confronting one of the chief obstacles to improving life in America.

The great challenge we are facing in education today is to harness the energy and dynamism of American society that has already transformed almost every industry and sector of our nation. Our challenge is to convince the public that many of the biggest problems in education stem from the teachers' unions' lust to hide failure, control funding, and target all those who expose the shortcomings in their established order.

2

COMPETING VISIONS
FOR AMERICAN EDUCATION

When the president of the United States asks you to be the US secretary of education, you don't just say no. And so, when the president-elect's team called to ask me to take this esteemed position, I accepted, knowing that the strong policy and communications background I had developed during my time as superintendent of the Houston school system could contribute to the president's plan to improve the nation's schools.

I was quite aware at the time (and even more so now, years later) that Washington was the most polarized and partisan place in America. But I knew I had a friend there. What you see in the president really is what you get. George W. Bush is one of the most authentic human beings I've ever had a chance to meet. What he says is what you can count on. It is how he lives his life, and it is how he governs.

I also knew, from the work he had done in Texas to transform the education system and create genuine accountability for results, that Bush would be serious about education reform during his time in Washington. History will likely remember this president for his leadership in the war on terror and his controversial decisions regarding Iraq. But I, and many others, will remember his vital stance on education.

As many people know, when he became governor of Texas in 1994, Mr. Bush led the way in implementing one of the best accountability systems in the country. Crafted and enacted with bipartisan support, it drew national attention and praise and set an example that other states (some of them, anyway) would try to emulate. As superintendent in Houston at the time, I was engaged in essentially the same struggle to create accountability, but on a local level. My beliefs about education reform were very much in sync with the president's.

There is a clear "theory of action" underlying the Bush administration's education policy agenda, and it is this: accountability, transparency, and choice are the keys to excellence in American education. I fully support this strategy, believing it is the best way to move our system out of the complacency and stagnation that has plagued it for so long.

Let's consider this theory of action more closely. First, *accountability*. What does this mean? It means that every person, and every part of our education system, needs to be held accountable for results—students and parents, teachers and principals, staff, school board members, superintendents, unions, and legislators. Everyone.

Second, *transparency*. We have to make sure that parents and taxpayers have solid, easily accessible, accurate information in order to judge whether their schools are succeeding or not, for all children. They have a right to know that.

And third, *choice*. Using this information about schools and school districts, parents must be allowed to choose the school that is best for their child. Choice is the ultimate step in accountability. When the education marketplace works as it should, unfettered by bureaucratic obstacles, good schools will flourish because they are successful at attracting students, and bad schools will perish, as they should. It works that way in any enterprise that is predicated on knowledgeable consumers making informed choices about what is best for them. The key, of course, is ensuring that consumers (parents and students) have the information they need to make informed choices.

President Bush and I agree on some other guiding principles, too. Both of us believe wholeheartedly in setting high standards for student achievement and making sure that students have every opportunity to meet them. Not a low bar for performance that everyone can reach, but a high bar that stretches children to their full potential. We both are deeply committed to identifying, confronting, and extinguishing failure—and, on the flip side, rewarding good schools and great teachers and determining how best to replicate their successes.

When Governor Bush came to Washington to become President Bush, he was determined to lead dramatic reform of our education system based on his theory of action. He had campaigned hard on that promise and fully intended to see it through. So when he invited me to be his secretary of education, I knew that a key part of my job would be helping him figure out how to do it.

Whether you agree with the provisions of No Child Left Behind or not, it would be hard to find anyone who says that the law was anything short of revolutionary. Until 8 January 2002, parents and taxpayers had little information about what was going on in education. The only measures that Americans had to determine the success or failure of the public schools came from periodic national tests such as the National Assessment of Educational Progress (NAEP) or international comparative studies such as the Third International Mathematics and Science Study (TIMSS) test. How could parents and taxpayers evaluate the quality of their local schools and school districts? And how could anyone tell how well schools were doing at closing or eliminating the achievement gap between minority and majority, rich and poor children? It wasn't possible. The data simply wasn't easily available.

Before the No Child Left Behind Act, America's education system was a well-funded failure.

- Since 1966, combined state, local, and federal government spending has topped more than $1 trillion.[1]
- Federal discretionary spending on education had more than doubled since 1996 and had subsequently surged 49 percent under the first four years of President George W. Bush alone.[2]
- Spending per pupil has skyrocketed over the last three decades— going from just over $3,000 a year to more than $8,194 a year.[3] In our nation's biggest districts, such as Washington DC, that number has reached more than $16,000 a year.[4]

Yet, despite this increased spending:

- Fewer than one-third of our fourth graders (and an equivalent proportion of our eighth graders) read proficiently.
- Reading performance has improved only slightly over the past fifteen years among fourth graders and has not improved at all among eighth graders.[5]
- Just 20 percent of our nation's seventeen-year-olds demonstrate proficiency in math.[6]
- And, among the industrialized nations of the world, American twelfth graders ranked near the bottom in science and math.[7]

These abysmal performance statistics simply confirmed what had long been suspected. Two decades earlier, in fact, the landmark study "A Nation at Risk" had sounded the alarm:

Our Nation is at risk. Our once unchallenged preeminence in commerce, industry, science, and technological innovation is being overtaken by competitors throughout the world. . . . If an unfriendly foreign power had attempted to impose on America the mediocre educational performance that exists today, we might well have viewed it as an act of war. As it stands, we have allowed this to happen to ourselves. . . . We have, in effect, been committing an act of unthinking, unilateral education disarmament.[8]

This assessment, written in April 1983, is one of the most potent warnings issued by a commission in US history. As the report intoned, "Our society and its education institutions seem to have lost sight of the basic purposes of schooling, and of the high expectations and disciplined effort needed to attain them."[9]

In response to this warning call, national groups and some states began to talk of standards-based reforms. There was a growing awareness that the status quo could not stand. But spending continued to climb without any significant results to show for it. And accountability was a foreign concept.

It was not until No Child Left Behind that increasing funding began to be linked with accountability and expectation of results. For the first time ever, NCLB required states to develop and implement statewide accountability systems. Specifically, they had to

- set academic standards in each content area for what students should know and be able to do;
- gather specific, objective data through tests aligned with those standards;
- use test data to identify strengths and weaknesses in the system;
- report school condition and progress to parents and communities;
- empower parents to take action based on school information;
- celebrate schools that make real progress; and
- direct changes in schools that need help.

For the first time, parents and taxpayers were ensured access to critical information that would allow them to judge the academic achievement of their children and the overall condition of schools, including safety and teacher quality. The president and I both believed that the passage of NCLB was an epic day in American education history. Now, real improvements in our schools would finally be possible, providing hope for every child.

THE UNIONS WAGE WAR ON NCLB

President Bush signed the No Child Left Behind Act into law 8 January 2002 with bipartisan support. But before the ink was even dry, the NEA had already voiced its strong objections to the law and vowed to do all within its power to stand in its way.

Why such a vehement reaction? I think the best way to answer that question is to reflect on teachers' unions' theory of action and how it compares with the "accountability, transparency, and choice" platform embraced by the Bush administration.

To the NEA and other change-resistant teachers' unions, accountability and transparency are not worthy goals. They are nefarious plots to embarrass and shame bad teachers. Union leaders are generally unwilling to admit that not all teachers are great at what they do. By saying this, I mean no disrespect against teachers. I believe that most of them—the vast majority, I would say—are outstanding, highly committed, wonderful people. But to suggest that none of them are bad, one would have to be delusional. That isn't true in any other profession, and cannot possibly be true in education either.

So, accountability and transparency are anathema to union leaders. What about choice? Chances are, if you're a national union leader, a defender of the status quo, you think that empowering parents to choose their children's schools is a terrible idea too. What if parents choose not to attend a particular school because the information they receive about its performance indicates that it is "bad" (e.g., poor performance, terrible achievement gap, unqualified teachers, etc.)?

Let's take this scenario a step further. When an accountability system like NCLB shows that a school is really bad, students are given the option to bail out of it. Isn't this desirable? Not to the NEA and its big friends in the union business. To them, opting out of a school can never be a good thing, because that bad school might have to close, which means that jobs would be lost (or job transfers would be necessary).

Instead, the teachers' union's solution would be to pour more money into that bad school—not to change practice within the building in order to earn a more desirable reputation. Whatever the problem is, more money is sure to be the answer. To a union, closing a school is unthinkable, even when enrollment patterns have changed and that school is no longer needed. Keep the school open and preserve those jobs. It's not about what students or parents or taxpayers need or want. It's about what the union wants: undiminished authority over jobs and money.

Let's sum this all up. What the Bush administration wants is accountability, transparency, and choice—a free market approach that puts parents in control of decisions about their children's education and provides them with the information they need to be good consumers. What recalcitrant unions want is to stifle accountability and choice, and perpetuate the myth that all schools and all teachers are equally good and all deserve to be fully protected. Clearly, these two paths were on a collision course from the moment that NCLB was signed into law. Conflict was inevitable.

Given this, it should come as no surprise that—true to its word—the NEA from Day One has been relentless in its efforts to undermine support for the law.

The NEA's legal and political battles against NCLB have been widely publicized. In 2005, for example, the NEA joined school districts in several states—including Texas, Michigan, and Vermont—in filing lawsuits against NCLB.

What is far less visible are the covert battles that the NEA has been waging against the law. As Joe Williams observed in a recent report, "the NEA has given millions of dollars to numerous organizations that have echoed [its] criticisms of NCLB. The union has supported independent partners that have waged publicity campaigns against NCLB, have encouraged their memberships to oppose NCLB, or have produced studies and articles critical of the law."[10]

Among the organizations with financial ties to the NEA, according to Williams, are advocacy groups like Communities for Quality Education and the Great Lakes Center for Education Research and Practice; union-funded research groups like the Harvard Civil Rights Project, the Economic Policy Institute, and the Keystone Research Center; political "bedfellows" like Americans for Democratic Action and the National Conference of Black Mayors; and civil rights groups such as the League of United Latin American Citizens.[11]

These types of connections, as Williams points out, are legal and commonplace. The big problem is the secretiveness of these arrangements. The NEA often does not disclose its financial ties to these organizations that share its opposition to NCLB. As a result, policymakers, the public, and the press are often deceived. When a parent reads a newspaper article or a report criticizing the law or its consequences, they may believe the source is impartial. But all too often, the source's financial ties to the NEA are simply hidden from the public's view.

Realizing the NEA's obvious determination to see NCLB fail, coupled with its enormous financial and communication power, those of us in the Department of Education were faced with a serious, two-phase challenge immediately after the law was enacted.

Phase One was that we had to achieve a timely and almost flawless implementation of one of the most complex education laws ever enacted by the Congress. Any error would be magnified a thousand times and used as evidence of the law's weakness and our ineptness.

Phase Two was that we had to design and implement a communication strategy to bring the public up to speed very quickly on a complex law that was the product of bipartisan negotiation. The law's effectiveness hinged on public participation, so we had to find ways to encourage parents and the public to participate in its programs and activities.

Both of these challenges were significant for a government bureaucracy that was not chartered, organized, funded, or staffed to conduct the type of communication and outreach efforts needed to even come close to matching the communication power of the NEA.

The vastly superior communication power of the NEA reminds me of one example in particular. In preparation for the 2003 congressional August recess, I met with Congressman John Boehner, chairman of the Workforce and Education Committee of the House of Representatives. John was a great ally in our communication cause. To this end, he had prepared a very attractive package of information about NCLB—including answers to frequently asked questions, an explanation of funding, and references where parents could go to get accurate information about NCLB. In addition, he included what parents could expect under the law and other very useful bits of information. The information was packaged in attractive color brochures, pamphlets, and even a DVD.

The idea was that members of Congress could take this information home with them during the August recess and conduct town hall meetings to help citizens understand the NCLB law. Many of them took advantage of this opportunity and sent out announcements in their congressional districts announcing the NCLB town hall meeting. Now, up to this point you would say that that's a very good idea, wouldn't you? Well, wait, as Paul Harvey would say, until you hear the rest of the story.

When many of the members of Congress arrived at the designated location of the town hall meetings for their districts, they found an unexpectedly large attendance. Imagine their hearts jumping for joy as they saw so many people interested in learning about NCLB! The story was the same from district to district. The meeting started. The representative put on a spirited presentation. They had their aides pass out the beautiful brochures and pamphlets. Then it was time for questions and answers.

Boom! The attentive crowd suddenly turned into an outraged mob as teacher after teacher stood to tell their sad story of how NCLB made their lives miserable. The perfectly designed propaganda poured out. The crowd joined in with sympathetic "Amens." And the members of Congress were hung out to dry. The meetings were a disaster. Multiply that by a large number of congressional district town hall meetings across the nation. Our worst nightmare at the Department of Education had been realized.

What happened? You have just witnessed a very small sample of the power of the NEA. When it learned of the town hall meetings from the announcements sent out by the congressional district offices, the NEA organized. They stacked the audiences with their members—usually local union stewards. During the question-and-answer period, these union stewards stood and introduced themselves as teachers, forgetting, of course, to disclose their affiliation and allegiance to the NEA.

The public related to them as teachers. The members of Congress were caught off guard as almost every statement they received from the audience was negative. The meeting ended, and the members of Congress staggered out and returned to Washington. The last thing they wanted to hear about ever again was NCLB—thus ceding the debate and public opinion to the one group that opposed any reform or debate about reform for the sake of our children or schools.

3

TEACHERS' UNIONS—WHAT THEY ARE
AND HOW THEY GOT THAT WAY

"NEA will become a political power
second to no other special interest group."

—NEA executive secretary Sam Lambert
NEA Journal, December 1967[1]

In the firestorm following my comment to the National Governors Association, many people from the National Education Association ridiculed the notion that I could make a distinction between teachers and their Washington-lobbyist leadership. For these activists, the interests of teachers' unions and teachers were one and the same, completely inseparable. But what was striking about nearly every one of the hostile letters was the fact that they did not point to any single, positive thing teachers' unions had accomplished. Nor did these letters mention how dysfunctional schools cripple the futures, or hinder the opportunities, of children.

Teachers' unions make many claims. They claim to be the compassionate and idealist protectors and stewards of the nation's children. They also claim to be the tough, resolute defenders of workers' rights.

And under this rubric, they claim to represent one of America's proudest civil traditions—the very idea of public education in a representative democracy.

We will address these claims in due course, for there is no shortage of critics, evidence, or former teachers who cast doubt on this valuable mythology. But in the divisive world of education, one thing is beyond debate: the teachers' union movement is a political powerhouse. The NEA and AFT are, arguably, the most influential unions in American history. The NEA has annual revenues of over one billion dollars and thousands of full-time, highly trained employees and activists.

Over the last ten years, teachers' unions have begun to surpass the AFL-CIO (American Federation of Labor and Congress of Industrial Organizations) in spending money on political campaigns, with tangible results.[2] In recent election years, one in eight delegates at the Democratic National Convention has been a member of a teachers' union—a larger contingent of delegates than produced by the electoral goldmine of California.[3]

As teachers' unions have grown in stature and influence, one would think that there would be a concomitant rise in educational achievement and quality—after all, the unions take great pains to remind us that they are indeed concerned about America's pupils. But this is one claim teachers' unions will not make. Over the last forty years, as teachers' unions' revenues and political influence have grown exponentially, educational performance has remained disappointing. Teachers' unions do not pass resolutions to make schools more accountable, reward teachers who do well, or pay more for teachers in high-demand fields, such as math and science.

Instead teachers' unions have succeeded in the first and most important goal—a goal boldly stated in 1967 by NEA Counsel Sam Lambert: the "NEA will become a political power second to no other special interest group."[4] Despite the persistent and obvious crisis in American education, the elite leadership of the teachers' unions has remained focused on this overriding political goal. And that has meant embracing techniques, tactics, policies, and positions that have almost nothing to do with improving American education.

As a July 2004 report by the Evergreen Freedom Foundation showed, the NEA may not have time to support merit pay for hardworking teachers, but they do have time for the following political activities:

- get-out-the-vote drives
- detailed political assessments and reports
- voter identification logs
- direct mass mailing
- email list-building
- providing publications from local, regional, state, and national affiliates
- contributions to candidates
- contributions to ballot initiatives
- paid political staff
- funding to political and ideological organizations
- funding to state affiliates
- coordinated campaigning with political parties
- NEA delegations at party conventions (state and national)
- phone banking, television, newspaper, and radio campaigns
- research and development
- polling
- purchase and operation of equipment[5]

As I said in my apology, there is a vast and abiding difference between teachers and lobbyists. The records show that the NEA uses its deep pockets and powerful lobby perch to campaign for issues like social security, gay rights, voting reform, immigration, the environment, abortion rights, urban development, socialized health care, and gun control, just to name a few.[6]

In 1994, the free-market Alexis de Tocqueville Institution tried to quantify the cost of all of the varied legislative issues that the NEA was supporting. It found that if all of the NEA's wish list was enacted, it would increase the size of the federal government by 40 percent, costing taxpayers an additional $702 billion, thereby increasing the yearly tax burden on an average family of four by $10,544.[7] Needless to say, its political agenda has only become more ambitious in the ten years since this study.

While debating all of these public policy issues is important for the future of America, these issues are at best only tangentially related and at worst a distraction from the NEA's first responsibility to improve education.[8]

The simple truth is, if ordinary citizens are to win the necessary battles for education reform, it is necessary to treat teachers' unions as powerful political operatives. Unfortunately, one of the reasons that teachers' unions are so arrogant and destructive is that many of their members are in total denial about their abuse of power politics. They think of themselves as being concerned professionals and idealists. However, this conflicting vision is the result of the union gaining so much power over such a short period of time. In order to effectively deal with these unions, an understanding of the history of teachers' unions and how they acquired their power is necessary.

How did an organization that is supposed to represent hardworking, idealistic teachers, who make around $48,000 a year (on average),[9] become Washington's most powerful political juggernaut? The purpose of this chapter is to show just how it happened.

HUMBLE ORIGINS AND EARLY RADICALIZATION

The NEA was founded in 1857, though it bore little resemblance to the leviathan organization it is today. In the beginning, it was little more than a handful of concerned educators. At that time, the NEA was primarily known for "coordinat[ing] state associations by providing an annual convention where ideas, theories and principles were discussed."[10] According to Charlene K. Haar, author of *The Politics of the PTA*, the NEA had only three appointed committees: one that recommended curricula for high school, one for youth education, and one that provided annual reports on enrollment, library resources, staff qualifications, and compensation.[11] In contrast to the American Federation of Teachers (AFT), a group affiliated with the AFL-CIO, the NEA began with an interest, not in power politics, but in professional concern with improving education at the local level. So prestigious was the group that many school boards required their teachers to join as a sign of the seriousness with which education was being treated by local officials.

This state and local focus was so deep that even decades later when the NEA became more directly involved in legislative advocacy, almost all of the group's advocacy work was confined to individual state legislatures, and teachers could voluntarily join the NEA either on the local, state, or national level. This was a very positive mission in many respects. Like other professional groups, the NEA worked to establish a national education policy, with agreed upon standards for teachers that began to emerge voluntarily as opposed to any heavy-handed imposition by the federal government to create policy. But what is especially noteworthy was that the NEA's motivation was to create professional standards and curricular excellence—a stark contrast to the union's current approach to teacher accountability and general indifference to scientifically based education research. In those early days, union members felt a professional sense of responsibility to children and the public that often caused them to put student instruction ahead of their own well-being, and drove them to hone good educational theories while discarding the bad.

In fact, for a long time after its inception, the NEA had virtually nothing in common with a traditional union. It was devoted to educational advocacy and professional excellence on a largely volunteer basis. To give you idea of how beneficial and benign the NEA was once considered, the NEA was given a congressional charter in 1906, and its Washington DC headquarters was given a special property-tax exemption. Only six other organizations were ever given such privileges: "the American Legion, the American National Red Cross, American War Mothers, AMVETS, Boy Scouts of America, and the Disabled American Veterans."[12]

The NEA is hardly a charitable organization in the sense that these other organizations are. Yet, even after it became both a union *and* a lobby, it continued to reap the benefits of its congressional charter. In 1996, after Congress had repeatedly threatened to revoke its property tax exemption, the NEA voluntarily agreed to begin paying 40 percent of the property tax it would owe without the exemption. (The annual property tax it would normally pay on its $80 million DC headquarters amounts to $2 million a year, or the dues of just seventeen thousand of its members.[13]) This cozy situation lasted until the late 1990s, when Congress finally decided to end the NEA's tax exemption.

But if the NEA was once considered harmless and charitable, all that began to change in the early part of this century. Around the same time that the NEA was receiving its federal charter, the AFT was founded as part of the American Federation of Labor (AFL) during a union movement that swept through the country like a tornado. The union movement soon proved to be a harbinger of a larger embrace of progressive politics that soon followed.

After the end of World War I, school enrollment began to explode across the country. The nation's growing school system needed more guidance than ever. But suddenly, the NEA and AFT both began to be more politically influential, moving outside the world of education. They both began to use their newfound power to push an overtly ideological agenda, heavily influenced by John Dewey—one of the most influential thinkers in modern education. However, in their rush to embrace Dewey, many forgot that he advocated socialism and endorsed the relatively new Soviet school system.

In the 1920s and '30s, partly in response to the Great Depression, the teachers' unions truly began following Dewey's lead. They began to view their mission not just as educators but as a collection of people who could fix society as a whole. At the NEA's 1934 annual meeting, Willard Givens, who served as the organization's executive secretary for fifteen years, gave a speech that contained the following remarks:

A dying laissez-faire must be completely destroyed and all of us, including the "owners," must be subjected to a large degree of social control. . . . The major function of the school is the social orientation of the individual. It must seek to give him understanding of the transition to a new social order.[14]

Even if it is rooted in a vision of an ideal society, this sentiment—that educators can "reorient" children to fulfill a radical ideological agenda—is a chilling sentiment and runs directly counter to the choices and freedoms that are so vital to American constitutional government. And Givens was not alone in these ideas. Well into the 1950s, speeches and writings show innumerable instances of teacher-union leadership embracing dangerous ideology. During this time, many of the country's academics were caught up in progressive politics.

Even today, teachers' unions continue to support aggressive ideological stances on social issues that have little to do with education—issues that few other unions persistently support. It is, therefore, not a stretch to say that because of education's leaning toward all things intellectual, these socialist-utopian ideas must have impacted teachers' unions more than most other labor organizations, with their patriotic, blue-collar leanings. In fact, this leftward drift, as well as the NEA's sense of infallibility, would have a major effect on driving the abusive power politics that teachers' unions would embrace in the next phase of their political evolution.

COLLECTIVE BARGAINING

Though not thought of as being overly influential in politics during the first half of the twentieth century, teachers' unions were quietly expanding their power, with their more left-wing leadership taking more stringent control of the organization's internal discourse and operations. The key accomplishment was the exclusion of the teachers' unions from provisions of the Hatch Act. The Hatch Act severely limited the amount of political activism that public employee unions could engage in. It took four years of lobbying, but in 1942, teachers' unions were excluded from the act's provisions.

Yet, despite this unprecedented protection, it would still be almost two more decades before teachers' unions made the big leap that would rock the political landscape and alter the future of the education system forever: a jump into collective bargaining. It is an issue that measures where our education debate stands; it is an issue that so many Americans believe that we do not spend enough time discussing. However, few Americans could truly define collective bargaining.

Put simply, collective bargaining happens when workers organize and appoint representatives to negotiate for better employment rights, benefits, wages, and work conditions. There are a number of advantages for individual workers who join unions and participate in collective bargaining. Individuals often do not have the time or resources to deal with management themselves; so, they let union leaders and labor professionals speak for them. However, as unions become increasingly large and political, they are less able to address the needs of individual workers. Everyone is either benefited or harmed collectively. If you disagree with union decisions, you often have no way to opt out. For instance, members have frequently had to sue their union to get back dues spent on political activity that they personally disagreed with.

Though no state expressly forbade collective bargaining for teachers, public opinion and political sentiment kept it from happening. After nearly fifty years of teachers' union members publicly advocating collective bargaining, the local union representatives in New York City, stirred by eager and dynamic organizers, began testing the waters and held a vote among union members. They overwhelmingly supported pursuing collective bargaining, sending shockwaves throughout the nation. This came about, in part, because the new Kennedy administration had made it clear that it would support unions as payback for their help in electing Kennedy in his extraordinarily close election. (As evidence of this, just a few months after teachers in New York began to move toward collective bargaining, Kennedy signed Executive Order 10988, allowing collective bargaining with federal employee unions—a major victory for the teachers' unions.[15])

Right from the start, the way the first union negotiations among teachers in New York were handled has had very negative consequences that still affect us today. A major part of the vote to support collective bargaining was to decide *who* should handle bargaining on the teachers' behalf. This was significant for a couple of reasons. First, at that time, the NEA and the AFT were structured very differently. The AFT was a "wall-to-wall" union, which means that it represented the interests of all teachers without making any distinctions about the subject they taught or what grade level they worked with. The NEA signed up teachers and divided them between high school, junior high, and elementary teachers and believed, at first, they should bargain as separate units.

The New York school board ended up consulting renowned labor relations expert Dr. George Taylor, from the University of

Pennsylvania. Taylor recommended dealing with all of the teachers collectively. So, the final vote came down to which union would represent teachers as a whole. Since the NEA had staked its claim on separate bargaining units, not surprisingly it lost by a two-to-one margin. There was quite a lot of media attention surrounding this decision, and it made quite a big impact on many future labor decisions. Had Taylor recommended separate bargaining units, that pattern might have continued in teachers' union negotiations to this day.[16]

But this election also had a secondary effect that isn't much discussed. The loss helped galvanize the NEA's more radical leadership at the expense of those who believed in the vision of professional responsibility. There had always been a rivalry between the AFT and NEA—which split on that vision—but the 1961 election brought another rift to the forefront. The NEA enrolled administrators as members, whereas the AFT did not. The AFT had long suspected that administrators who were NEA members had been imposing undue influence on those under their charge, pressing them to join the NEA instead of the AFT.

Led by an AFT organizer named Walter Ruether, the AFT was resolved to do everything they could to poach NEA membership—in fact, half of the local AFT's membership had enrolled in the year prior to the representation and collective bargaining vote. This rivalry reached its apex during the ramp-up to the representation vote, where the AFT went so far as to employ a spy in the NEA's office.[17] In the end, the local AFT received just over twenty thousand votes in favor of their representation, despite the fact that it enrolled only 5,200 members, the discrepancy coming in large part from NEA members who voted against their own union.[18] The NEA had reason to be worried.

After the loss, William G. Carr, the NEA's executive director, viewed this leap forward in unionism as potentially devastating: "This . . . is the first time in which forces of significant scope and power are considering measures which could destroy the Association."[19] Carr was partly right. The vote did not destroy the organization, just its vision of professional responsibility to improve education.

It was one of the rare moments when everyone involved knew history was being made. Both sides correctly identified the shift to collective bargaining in New York as an event that would determine the future of education. Even today, the general public knows little about what collective bargaining means. It affects every aspect of public education, especially because teachers' unions possess the money to buy power and the political means to undermine nearly every reform.

In the short term, however, the two organizations knew that one of them could easily face extinction. The union that was viewed as less effective in the collective-bargaining process risked becoming irrelevant. From the outset, the NEA appeared to be at a distinct disadvantage. Though it had been acting as a de facto union for some time, in the early '60s it still had the veneer of its history as an all-around educational association, whereas the AFT had been a hard-core union since its inception and was therefore seen as better prepared to deal with employment-related matters.

With the historic vote signaling the future, the NEA adjusted quickly to the new realities. At first, the NEA tried to capitalize on its prior reputation to make the AFT look bad as it aggressively pursued collective bargaining for its members elsewhere in the country. In 1964, when the Newark Teachers Union, an AFT affiliate, went on strike, the NEA denounced it as unwarranted and irresponsible. Two years later, the Newark Teachers Association, an NEA affiliate, won representation rights and went on strike. This time, the NEA was quick to point out that it didn't have an official strike policy. By the end of the decade, the NEA was fully in support of teachers' rights to strike. It has never looked back.[20]

However, the fact that in a few short years the NEA totally discarded its century-old reputation as an organization dedicated to improving all facets of education through professional cooperation and learning is only half the story. The other part of the saga is how power politics was melded into the radical organization it became.

By the 1970s, strikes were no longer a matter of righting wrongs or addressing grievances—the NEA viewed them as a means to an end. The most telling indicator of this shift occurred when the NEA began using Saul Alinsky as a consultant. Alinsky gained considerable fame as an organizer in the late 1960s and is perhaps best known for his book *Rules for Radicals*, published in 1971. (The book infamously opened with an acknowledgement to Lucifer.)

Alinsky personally conducted intense training sessions with the NEA's field organizers (known as UniServ operatives), until his unexpected death in 1972. His influence over the NEA was felt almost immediately, and while his efficacy as an organizer is undisputed, his means remain highly controversial. Alinsky explicitly believed that the ends do, in fact, justify the means. Here are some sentiments on "ethics" from *Rules for Radicals*:

- One's concern with the ethics of means and ends varies inversely with one's personal interest in the issue.
- In war the end justifies almost any means.
- Concern with ethics increases with the number of means available and vice versa.
- Generally, success or failure is a mighty determinant of ethics.
- The morality of means depends upon whether the means is being employed at a time of imminent defeat or imminent victory.
- You do what you can with what you have and clothe it in moral garments.
- Pick a target, freeze it, personalize it, polarize it.
- The judgment of the ethics of the means is dependent on the political position of those sitting in judgment.

- If you push a negative hard enough and deep enough, it will break through to its counter-side.[21]

It is widely accepted and acknowledged that Alinsky had a profound impact on NEA operations. In fact, the NEA still uses his training manuals, and one of their own internal memoranda contains the following: "Generally, the Alinsky advice on tactics is guerilla war advice. To win: know the enemy, divide the enemy, know who all the players are, conduct the action on several levels, and personalize the conflict."[22]

As secretary of education and a big city superintendent, I got to see, firsthand, the personalization of conflict described.

Of course, in the Alinsky worldview, the enemy ends up being anyone who gets in the way. The fact that teachers' unions have subscribed to these tactics should be a source of deep sadness to any American who believes schools and teachers should serve children and parents and not the other way around. The Alinsky tactics have led to a merciless defense of the status quo and to a radical, confrontational approach that cannot be stopped because of the power of monopoly gained through the collective bargaining process.

Collective bargaining has, in effect, shut out parents from having a say in their local schools. The Alinsky tactic of "personaliz[ing] the conflict" has driven the education establishment to ridicule and savage those few parents who do speak up—often calling them "extremists," "religious ideologues," "right-wing conservatives," and other intended epithets. Many a liberal parent whose child was falling behind has been surprised by such attacks when they dared to speak up.

Collective bargaining has rendered the Parent Teacher Association (PTA) almost useless as a representative of parents' needs. This is a somewhat practical consideration by the PTA in the face of collective bargaining monopolies. It's hard enough to come to an agreement with two opposing sides in a labor dispute, let alone three. Even acknowledging that the PTA has never been much more than a "coffee and cookies" organization, in 1965, before collective bargaining became firmly entrenched, PTA membership was ten times that of both major teachers' unions combined. The PTA was a force to be reckoned with. But as teacher strikes became more common, the PTA had a real dilemma on its hands. Early PTA attempts at manning and staffing schools during strikes, to ensure the safety of children, were met with outright hostility, and teachers were branded as strikebreakers. (Of course, unions fought to keep schools closed, as it was in their best interest to burden the parents and threaten their ability to work when they must be looking after their children. This tactic put tremendous pressure on school boards to resolve the dispute quickly by caving in and unburdening the community.) And if the PTA in any way threatened to side with the school board, the teachers threatened to withdraw membership. By the end of the 1960s, the PTA had officially adopted a policy of neutrality.[23]

This neutrality hasn't kept concerned parents from fighting teachers' unions, but teachers' unions have been exceedingly harsh in dealing with dissent from the PTA. In 1976, the PTA and the Ohio Education Association (an NEA affiliate) went head-to-head over three bills in the state legislature. One of the bills was regarding labor relations and strong arbitration guidelines; the other two were about regulating teacher qualifications and grounds for dismissal. The PTA won, on paper. But later that year, due to a campaign by the OEA and the withdrawal of the union's teachers from the organization, fifty thousand members quit, nearly crippling Ohio's PTA.[24]

The emphasis on power politics in such cases has made the message crystal clear. Get in the way of the teachers' unions and there will be retribution. It will be swift, and it will be harsh. Just fifteen years after the advent of collective bargaining, the teachers' unions had resources and tactics that essentially neutralized both school boards and the PTA—traditionally the two major checks on their power at a local level. It was time to attack much bigger obstacles in achieving total power over education.

THE POLITICAL ERA

A decade after collective bargaining originated, teachers' union rhetoric began to undergo a dramatic shift. The NEA in particular had always viewed the education debate and the creation of policy as issues worthy of national discussion. As was stated earlier, it was a clear driving force in founding the organization in the mid-nineteenth century. But since education was traditionally governed and funded by local authorities, it remained an issue that largely escaped the purview of national politics. Education is hardly a one-size-fits-all issue, and there are clear advantages in leaving educational control in the hands of local school boards and parents. However, this was a *hindrance* for unions and their special interests. Rather than fight the same battle in thousands of school districts, teachers' unions knew it would be much easier to simply have Congress pass laws that compelled all states to comply. So the teachers' unions simply set out to control education at the source of political power, at the top of the federalist structure.

In 1974, NEA president Helen Wise flatly enunciated a new ideological dictum: "We must reorder Congressional priorities by reordering Congress. We must defeat those who oppose our goals."[25] Wishing to have more of a say in national politics was hardly a new sentiment for the NEA; but in the past, such statements would have been more along the lines of thoughtful curricula discussions rather than a call to arms with marching orders by General Alinsky.

By the time that Wise made this comment, the threat to unseat politicians opposed to the NEA was real, even to the most respected leaders. As collective bargaining emerged as the main driving force of public education, union enrollment had grown exponentially. By 1965, just three years after the collective-bargaining victory in New York, the AFT's membership nearly doubled, and the NEA's membership increased by almost two hundred thousand.[26]

The major effect of this dramatic increase in enrollment was obvious. More members meant more dues. More money meant the teachers' unions could finally expand the scope of their organizations into the cutthroat world of national politics, to buy and support allies who would rewrite all the rules for them. In the past, teachers' unions kept their political lobbying efforts limited to specific pieces of legislation; now, they were proposing something much more ambitious, diving headfirst into electoral politics. The teachers' unions' early endeavors into politics were hardly inauspicious.

In 1976, the NEA issued its first formal endorsement of a presidential candidate—Jimmy Carter. But that was just the tip of the iceberg. That same election year, of the 323 House candidates the NEA endorsed, 272 won; of the 26 endorsed Senate candidates, 19 won. Almost over the course of one November night in 1976, the NEA made itself a force to be reckoned with, one that had few equals in Washington.[27]

The NEA's blatant attempts to grab power alarmed more than just a few people who could clearly see what the NEA's true goals were. At a 1976 rally in Florida, future president Ronald Reagan told the crowd that the NEA wanted "a federal education system . . . so that little Willie's mother would not be able to go down and see the principal or even the school board. She'd actually have to take her case to the Congress in Washington. I believe this is the road to disaster and the end of academic freedom."[28]

Though this may first seem like political hyperbole, The Gipper was as farsighted and visionary, as usual, as when spotting an ideological bloc of power. A few months after Reagan's statement, the 1976 election firmly entrenched the NEA in the Democratic power base. During that time, the NEA became almost mad with power. In remarks to the NEA convention in 1978, NEA executive director Terry Herndon gave a speech in which he described the NEA's goal: "to tap the legal, political and economic powers of the US Congress. We want leaders and staff with sufficient clout that they may roam the halls of Congress and collect votes and reorder the priorities of the United States of America."[29]

Notice he did not say *educational* priorities of the United States. Notice that he never mentioned children or the achievement gap or accountability. If this had been the stated goal of just about any other lobbying group, its sinister Orwellian tone would have been plastered across every front page in the country. Of course, it's almost hard to blame the NEA for being so cocky, especially when education reform came so easy.

In 1979, Jimmy Carter helped establish the federal Department of Education, despite the concept being opposed; it was almost unbelievable to modern eyes, by the *Washington Post* and most mainstream opinion outlets of the day. A major federal agency dedicated to education issues and policy had been a stated goal of the teachers' unions for decades. Carter had promised one in his campaign, and it had helped secure the NEA's endorsement.[30]

This was a major victory for the unions, but sadly, not necessarily one for quality education (this is something that, unfortunately, I know firsthand). It started with a less-than-modest budget of $14 billion. It now has a discretionary budget authority of over $57 billion.[31] Establishing the Department of Education, in line with the vision of the teachers' unions, has resulted in more federal bureaucracy, higher taxes, elimination of local control over education, and ultimately, worse schools. However, centralizing control over education made it easier for the unions to pull the necessary strings and accumulate power because no one else could amass the money or manpower to compete. Not until the No Child Left Behind Act did the federal government ask for concrete results or accountability for all the money that was being spent.

Carter only lasted long enough to entrench the teachers' unions' base of power and oversee the creation of the US Department of Education. So, despite Reagan's victory in 1980, the NEA went on the offensive—not just in supporting favorable candidates but in expressing ideological rhetoric as well. The teachers' unions were not about to go quietly into the night. In 1979, at the NEA's annual conference on Human and Civil Rights, the keynote speech was on the "Rise of the New Right." Even though roughly 60 percent of teachers' union members were registered Republicans or Independents, the NEA presumed to speak for its members in sweeping ideological terms.[32]

In 1982, the NEA sued Suzanne Clark, the author of a book critical of the NEA, *Blackboard Blackmail*. In deposition testimony, the president of the NEA confirmed that it would be accurate to say that NEA had "declared war against the new right," and NEA employee Dorothy Massie admitted that she kept about twelve file drawers dedicated to keeping tabs on conservative political groups.[33] The politicization of the NEA was effectively complete. There was little pretense that the NEA was dedicated to coming up with the best solutions for education. They were focused on only two things: Mission One was to oppose, destroy, and defeat their critics at the polls. Mission Two was to dedicate themselves to advancing a radical agenda—one that rarely mentioned children, never gave parents power, and rarely held teachers accountable or measured the results of their control over schools.

By this time the damage was essentially irreparable—teachers' unions weren't acting in good faith toward students and education policy, and everyone knew it. In 1983, the *American School Board Journal* ran a column expressing these frustrations:

Everyone knows it's true, of course, but we prefer the teacher unions to say it in their own words. Notes a bulletin sent to teachers from a local chapter of the Oregon Education Association (an NEA affiliate): "The major purpose of our association is not education, rather it ought to be the extension and/or preservation of our members' rights. We earnestly care about kids and learning, but that is secondary to other goals".[34]

But the NEA was so powerful that even Reagan knew better than to try to tackle both the Soviet empire and the teachers' unions' grip on their education monopoly at the same time. Perhaps fearing reprisal, he appointed an education insider with strong ties to the NEA, Terrel Bell, as his first secretary of education. In his memoirs, *The Thirteenth Man*, Bell makes it clear that he was opposed to any serious reform—especially the idea that the Department of Education should be abolished, a promise that Reagan had made during his campaign. While serving as secretary of education, Bell asked the president to appoint an independent commission to study the state of American education as an attempt to publicly demonstrate the value of the Department of Education. When Reagan declined to indulge Bell, Bell went ahead and prepared his infamous "A Nation at Risk" report as a way of doing an end run around Reagan's wishes.[35]

The report pointed out the obvious, which was that educational standards had been falling. But the report was blatantly political. Reagan's chief vulnerability during his first few years in office was the economy, which was still staggering from Carter's disastrous administration. "A Nation at Risk" tried to blame poor education for the country's bad economic situation.[36] Writing in the journal *Education Next*, Diane Ravitch assesses the report's conclusions thus:

It seems clear that the report's attempt to draw a straight line between the quality of the schools and the health of the economy was on shaky ground. It would be ridiculous to claim that a nation's economic well-being is unaffected by the quality of education available to its citizens. But the connections are not as clear-cut as *Risk* asserted, and there are many other factors . . . that can compensate for the failings of the for-mal K-12 system.[37]

If Ravitch's earnest academic tone is to be believed, in retrospect, it is also accepted that "the roots of *Risk* began in an effort to salvage the US Department of Education" and that "while [the report's] findings were dead on, its reform agenda relied too much on the existing sys-tem."[38] Reagan simply could not be seen as attacking the Department of Education when both the nation's children and economy were so vulnerable.

Of course, it didn't matter that Bell had essentially set up a giant straw-man. The report never questioned failing educational standards as a result of the concurrent rise in federalization and unionization that took away from local and state authorities over education. Since Bell successfully preserved the Department of Education, education spend-ing and the size of the education bureaucracy is at an all-time high. Yet academic performance has only recently become an issue of debate. The fact that the economy has steadily improved every year since the report was released only proves that the system is failing students, not that Americans aren't as capable as ever. (Imagine our economic potential if we had a world-class education system that served every child—not just an elite few.)

The only possible explanation of Bell's appointment and the ensu-ing fiasco is that Reagan feared union reprisal at the ballot box. Two weeks after he was inaugurated for his second term, Reagan dumped Bell. He appointed the former head of the National Endowment for the Humanities, William Bennett, as secretary of education. Bennett is known for being utterly unambiguous about the failings of the modern education system. According to Bennett:

I think the NEA is one of the most reprehensible organizations within the law. There are some illegal organizations that are worse in the

United States. It is opposed to every serious educational reform. It puts its own interest ahead of the children. It has complained so bitterly about the teaching profession that it has discouraged many people from going into teaching.[39]

Still, as much as a firebrand as Bennett was (and still is), the NEA and the education bureaucracy survived his formidable rhetorical tempests. In the end, zero progress was made in cutting it down to size. Reagan's promise to shut down the Department of Education and give parents and local communities more control over education only existed as a dream of the Great Liberator.

When President Bill Clinton came into office, the first Democrat since Carter, it almost didn't seem possible that teachers' unions could be any more powerful. They survived one of the most popular presidents and a sworn enemy. When Clinton got elected in 1992, he eked by in a three-way race with one of the lowest vote totals in modern history. He didn't forget who helped put him there. For years, teachers' unions had been giving the Democratic Party tens of millions of dollars—money and manpower that has become integral to the success of Democratic air and ground operations at election time. Both parties have their special interests. But in the GOP, it is hard to point to lobbies so fiercely protected by law and government power. And while most businesses split their donations between the parties (despite most media reports to the contrary), it's not uncommon for 99 percent of the NEA's political action committee (PAC) money to go to only Democratic candidates. By contrast, the staunchly conservative National Rifle Association still manages to give almost a quarter of its PAC money to aid in electing Democrats.[40]

Attending the NEA's annual convention in 1993, President Clinton thanked the NEA "for the gift of our assistant secretary," referring to the newly appointed Department of Education assistant secretary Sharon Robinson, a longtime NEA employee and activist. Clinton then told the crowd at the convention, "You and I are joined in a common cause, and I believe we will succeed."[41] If by common cause, he means failing America's children, I congratulate them on their success. The Clinton administration's ties continued to be strengthened. Six months later, after Clinton's admission, Debra DeLee, director of governmental relations for the NEA, left her job to become executive director of the Democratic National Committee.

The Clinton administration seemed willing to aid and abet the NEA's stated goal of influencing politics directly. All political machinations, especially in the wake of an election, involve some unfortunate degree of patronage. But to truly put this in perspective, pass this by the "NRA Test." Would the public or media not be outraged by the appointment of a high-level NRA employee and activist if he were given a plum position at the Bureau of Alcohol, Tobacco, and Firearms? Surely his résumé would indicate he knows something about firearms, but many voters would be right to question if his ideological bias would cause him to act in a way that is not representative of all Americans. Would not the RNC being run by the NRA's head lobbyist be a source of public scrutiny? Yet for some reason this behavior with regard to the Democrats and the NEA goes unquestioned.

This was the story of the Clinton years. Clinton's no-nonsense political operatives spoke passionately about education when it was to their advantage, to attack House Speaker Newt Gingrich and the Republicans in Congress. But over those eight years, they did nothing to extend the promise of education to every child. The culmination of the NEA's final goal—literally fusing itself with government authority, the Democratic Party, and electoral politics so as to render its wishes indistinguishable from the other—was the unfortunate legacy of the Department of Education that President George W. Bush inherited.

4

CUTTING DOWN OUR BEST TEACHERS AND SLASHING THEIR PAY

Senator John Kerry was hot on the presidential campaign trail traveling through the heartland of America when, on 3 May 2004, he took a risky political step. In the midst of baling hay and sampling chili, the Democratic hopeful devised a fresh, new idea. The Kerry campaign issued a press release that barely registered as a blip on the media's radar screen, but for the teachers' unions it looked like the first wave of a nuclear strike.

On that warm spring day, the Kerry Campaign issued a simple press release stating that Democratic presidential candidate John Kerry supported new systems that reward teachers for excellence in the classroom, including pay based on improvement in student achievement.[1]

It was a simple, fair, and revolutionary idea: reward good teachers, encourage our best and brightest to stay in the profession, and put talented, experienced instructors in failing schools where they are needed the most.

For parents and voters, it is one of the most popular ideas in politics. When the idea comes up, the first thing that comes to mind is that one, young dynamic teacher who puts in the extra hours, shows that extra enthusiasm, and reaches out to ensure every child is learning. This simple, fair, and revolutionary idea is, however, the most dangerous threat to teachers' unions.

John Kerry learned this lesson the hard way. To his credit, the Kerry campaign correctly identified low pay for great teachers as a major barrier to improving public education—it robs teachers of their initiative; prevents principals, parents, and the public from rewarding those teachers who set an example for the whole system; and, in many cases, it causes unions and poor teachers to pressure and harass teachers who go that extra mile. In unfolding their education platform, the Kerry campaign proposed a $30 billion, ten-year federal-grant program, which would allow school districts to increase the pay of teachers whose students consistently perform above average. Referring to teachers, candidate John Kerry said that "greater achievement ought to be a goal," but that merit pay ought to work "just the way it does in every other sector of professional employment."[2]

The National Education Association sprung to action almost immediately. The NEA pulled Kerry off the campaign trail to express its fury with his remarks. But within weeks (allowing for enough time to cloak the appearance of an immediate flip-flop), NEA president Reg Weaver referred to a "very positive meeting" with the candidate. In the 21 May 2004 memo, which was obtained by the always-enterprising Education Intelligence Agency, Weaver admitted that the NEA got the kind of assurances it demands of every Democrat. He reported in an almost sinister understatement that Senator Kerry "clarified that the campaign did not intend to use that language [supporting merit pay] and would not do so in the future."[3]

Why is it that teachers' unions so strongly object to the idea of good pay for great teachers? After all, parents and voters don't just support it; they are overwhelmingly in favor of it. Few ideas garner more support in public debate than merit pay. The centrist-oriented

Democratic Leadership Council conducted a poll asking the simple question whether we should be "paying teachers not based on seniority, but based on the value that they bring to the classrooms, as measured by improvements in their students' test scores."[4] Two out of three voters (66 percent) *strongly supported* the idea. Another 18 percent *somewhat supported* the idea of rewarding great teachers. Combined, support for merit pay came to 84 percent! Almost no public policy idea has attracted this much bipartisan support. In addition to these results, 60 percent of Democrats *strongly* supported performance pay, with 65 percent of Republicans and 73 percent of Independents also being strong backers of this idea. Include those who "somewhat support" performance pay, and support surges to 79 percent for Democrats, 79 percent for Republicans, and an astronomical 92 percent from Independents.[5] Based on results like these, it is clear there is a desire for change.

But when state and local officials finally realize that the public wants our nation's best teachers paid for the quality of their work, the system will never be the same. That's why teachers' unions must do all they can to keep this issue from becoming a debate. This is why John Kerry was ordered by the NEA to stay after school and forced to write, "I will not speak out of turn," on the chalkboard one hundred times.

The truth is, performance pay threatens the teachers' unions' monopoly over their members. Thus, teachers must be indiscriminately lumped together, their pay must be the same, and any teacher, no matter how good, who voices any dissent or does any extra work beyond the minimum outlined by contract, must be punished. The grim reality of modern education politics is that teachers' unions hold their members and their political servants accountable for any deviation from the established party line. Meanwhile, teachers have little recourse to hold the unions accountable—or to even know what is going on with their dues. To cloak this brutal *realpolitik*, teachers' unions maintain that they are the sole force protecting teachers and fighting to increase their pay.

But too few teachers challenge this line of thinking.

In an article for *Government Union Review*, Paul E. Peterson, the director of Harvard's Program on Education Policy and Governance, asked a simple question: "If their unions are so powerful, why are teachers not better paid?"[6] Peterson suffers no illusions about a group that can call a presidential candidate to heel: "Teacher union power is awesomely arrogant."[7] With such unequalled influence, Peterson adds, "Powerful unions should be generating high wages that attract the best and brightest. Yet pay and ability are going the same direction as Wrong-Way Corrigan."[8]

This is because union officials demand, and get, uniform pay for all teachers. This is preposterous. Uniform pay may be less objectionable in, say, a factory situation, where one person can easily substitute for another on an assembly line, and there is almost no perceptible difference in job performance. However, teaching is a profession that is specialized; it requires a great deal of adaptability, and the responsibilities are far too important to pretend that all teachers are equal.

The lack of "merit pay" ensures that the best and brightest steer clear of the education profession. Peterson points out that in the last fifty years, teacher pay, relative to private sector salaries, has declined substantially.[9] Talented people that once might have considered teaching have little incentive to enter a system that pays them far less than their abilities are worth on the open market.

BAD TEACHERS IN, GOOD TEACHERS OUT

If the lack of financial incentives discourages good candidates from entering the teaching profession, what about those who do go into teaching? It is a testament to America that thousands of wonderful citizens still decide to become teachers, despite the perverse incentives and union-created obstacles. Many remain in public schools with a dedication and fortitude that is inspiring.

In my extensive travels as secretary of education, visiting schools throughout nearly every state in the union, I was always reminded of just how much we owe teachers—the soldiers of democracy. Like so many American parents, I wish we could pay those great teachers more to encourage everyone to work harder. I am proud to have been part of President Bush's efforts to support teachers—in particular, our efforts to provide teachers with liability protections against lawyers, such as when a teacher tries to preserve order and discipline. In addition, I am proud to have worked to get teachers help with their taxes, especially for all those times when dedicated teachers dipped into their own pockets to pay for school supplies. In both cases, great teachers are always thinking about the environment and expectations in which a child is taught—and such quality control and attention deserve our utmost honor, recognition, and rewards.

CREATING A CULTURE OF LEARNING

Consider for a moment just how difficult it can be for principals and school boards to reward the best teachers. The energy, money, and legal headaches that come with any attempt to remove an incompetent educator are truly mind-boggling.

In one infamous incident in South Carolina in 1981, a school tried to fire a teacher. The reason? Pure incompetence. At a hearing to determine her fitness to teach, she was given a ten-word vocabulary test. She incorrectly pronounced and was unable to define the word *agrarian*. She defined *suffrage* as "people suffering for some reason or other." She defined *ratify* as "to get rid of something." She excused her total lack of ability by saying, "I don't think I was the best, but I don't think that I did more harm than anyone else."[10]

What happened to this teacher in the face of overwhelming evidence that she was unqualified to teach? A judge ordered her reinstated.[11] Because of teachers' union lobbying, the contractual protections for teachers were so expansive that the local school board and principal were completely powerless in dealing with even this most incompetent of employees. This is too often the case.

Even more disgusting is the fact that the unions insist on defending such incompetence. The Texas State Teachers Association seems to have never met a teacher it would not defend from termination. The case of a lascivious drama teacher is illustrative. Nine female students who participated in this teacher's drama program accused the teacher of telling graphic stories about his sex life, including pointing out to his students the area where his girlfriend had "gone down on him"; repeatedly fondling his students' breasts; asking female students to try on sexy clothes in front of him, including a see-through dress and a bikini; telling students he wanted to date them when they turned eighteen; forcing students to rub his back; and telling one girl if she didn't stop struggling to get away from him he would "touch something she didn't want him to touch."[12]

Still the teachers' union defended this teacher, even though: 1) he did not show up for his termination hearing, 2) he pled the fifth to every question in the deposition concerning the charges, and 3) no exculpatory evidence was presented. Fortunately, the hearing examiner concluded that the case required "no careful distinctions between right and wrong," and the lascivious drama teacher's termination was upheld.[13]

Not even extreme cases of moral turpitude will get some teachers' unions to back off from defending teachers and unnecessarily tying up limited school resources in expensive hearings.

In Chicago, for example, the Chicago Teachers Association went on the attack when a group of teachers was caught helping their students cheat on a skills test. Rather than accept responsibility for the teachers' actions, the union president blamed district administrators for relying too much on tests and accused principals of pressuring teachers to produce high scores.[14] Schools chief Arne Duncan replied, "There is no justification for cheating. The vast majority of our teachers are helping our children learn not only the curriculum, but also right from wrong."

These examples are deplorable. But few positions are more damaging to children, to teachers, or to the nation's education system than teachers' union opposition to rewarding the best teachers. As unions became more powerful in traditionally run schools, collective bargaining required that unions bargain for *everyone*. To allow any choice in union representation, or to allow competing organizations to exist, would threaten that collective-bargaining position. "Solidarity" demanded, therefore, that every teacher, whether high school or kindergarten, whether a talented engineer teaching math or a physical education major teaching physical education, be paid the same.

As a student of organization and systems management, I agree with Peter Drucker. Few things are more important to defining the mission and success of an organization than who gets promoted and who get fired. As Drucker writes,

> As we have known for a long time, people in organizations tend to behave as they see others being rewarded. . . . Executives who do not make the effort to get their people decisions right do more than risk poor performance. They risk their organization's respect.[15]

That's exactly what happens with public confidence in our schools. The teachers' unions' protection of incompetence is crippling. As Peterson puts it, "Ask any urban superintendent how many teachers have been dismissed for reasons other than proven moral turpitude. The number is generally smaller than Roger Clemens' earned run average."[16] As one of those urban superintendents (in Houston's Independent School District), I can vouch for the truth of that statement. As US secretary of education, few things were more frustrating than meeting an outstanding principal, or an aspiring board member or superintendent, who could not turn his or her school around because of the incompetence of a few bad teachers and their phalanx of union accomplices. It was, and still is, most devastating to see the vast majority of teachers—those who are dedicated to education—suffer because of the incompetent few. What's worse, teachers' unions rarely, if ever, take a responsible position in supporting the mission of education. They almost always choose to protect the worst employees, and they seldom help identify, or attempt to hold accountable, the worst teachers. In my opinion, this is the single most incontrovertible and undeniable piece of evidence that unions are about power, and not pupils. The opposition to rewarding good teachers, and holding the bad teachers accountable, shows contempt for children's needs, parents' best hopes, and the principles of a good, honest government.

The simple lack of hiring-and-firing ability carries with it other liabilities. It puts an unnecessary burden on the best administrators. Jorge Izquierdo, a New York City principal, who was one of the few education professionals willing to speak out on the issue, put it this way: "I am like the CEO of a little corporation. I am judged by whether or not I achieve the equivalent of a profit—how much the children gain in learning. But unlike any other CEO, I can't hire the people who work here or fire them when they're incompetent."[17] Again, Izquierdo innately knows what acclaimed management expert Peter Drucker identifies as a major obstacle to running any organization: "Making the right people decisions is the ultimate means of controlling an organization well. Such decisions reveal how competent management is, what its values are, and whether it takes its job seriously."[18] But while unions fight attempts to keep teachers from being "controlled," fighting over school control isn't necessarily what hiring and firing are all about. Without that power, many teachers just wouldn't take their jobs seriously. The hope is not that teachers can be controlled, but that they will take their jobs seriously and ultimately do a good job as a way of being accountable to themselves.

Whether intended or not, the teachers' unions have created a system with a perverse set of incentives: not only is taxpayers' money directed away from good teachers, whose focus is ability and results, but it is directed toward the few bad teachers who are rewarded, starving the system of badly needed funds and debilitating the core mission of our schools. Of course, these contractual protections for the worst teachers would not exist if they did not benefit teachers' unions. The more contractual protections, the more bad teachers remain in the system. The more bad teachers remain in the system, the more parents and administrators complain. The more complaints there are against teachers, the more those teachers are dependent upon their union for protection. The vicious cycle is complete; students continue to suffer under teachers who sometimes have a worse vocabulary than they do, or a work ethic that translates into broken dreams for kids hoping to escape real-life nightmares.

However, when it comes to firing bad teachers, simply proving obvious incompetence is far from the biggest obstacle that administrators and school boards face. Union protection and teacher contracts are so extensive that getting through the job hearings and due-process protections built into their contracts is very expensive and time consuming. One scholar who studied the problem of firing teachers in the 1980s found that several administrators put away at least $50,000 *per teacher* to cover the legal and administrative costs of firing them.[19] Of course in certain extreme cases, that's not nearly enough.

- In San Diego, it took one school district four years to fire a teacher named Juliet Ellery, despite an abundance of complaints. Ellery fought the case for eight years afterward (and even tried to get the Supreme Court to hear her case). Ultimately, it cost the school district and taxpayers over $300,000 in legal fees. Ellery's license was suspended for only one year.[20]

- In New York, the average cost of firing a teacher is over $200,000. In one infamous New York case, a teacher collected his salary in prison for several years after he was convicted for selling cocaine, while the school district was still going through the due process requirements to fire him. That's right—it is easier to put a teacher in jail than fire him.[21]

- In his book *The Incompetent Teacher,* Stanford professor Edwin M. Bridges publishes an actual state of California memorandum detailing the expenses related to the firing of one teacher—to the tune of $166,715. In addition to paying the lawyer, this includes everything from paying for expert testimony, the hearing location, the court reporter, and salary for a substitute teacher while the case was being tried.[22]

In many of these cases, if the school board is unlucky enough to lose, they end up paying the teacher's legal fees as well. This is an important point because if a teacher is lucky enough to win a wrongful termination suit, far more often than not, this is not because they haven't been proven incompetent, but rather, the school board unintentionally violated some minute part of the sweetheart union-negotiated contract. This once again shows how teachers' unions are, in fact, sitting on both sides of the negotiating table, while parents and children have been locked out of the room. If a school board is engaged in a wrongful termination suit, it is an almost absolute certainty that the school board is in the right, because the cost and barriers to firing a teacher are so high that it is a huge risk for them. The teacher, on the other hand, has everything to gain, and the union has lots of cash and resources eager to justify their existence.

Obviously administrators and school boards are in a bind under this system. They cannot afford to reward the best teachers because they cannot fire the worst. The most common response is to ignore the incompetent teacher's problem and just hope that the problem goes away. There's only so much that administrators can do. If action is to take place, it has to become an issue with parents, particularly ones who are savvy enough to put political pressure on the school board or administrators before anyone does anything else. In suburban areas, where schools are usually better, the smaller schools and districts make it possible for parental and public pressure to be felt. But in larger, urban districts, school boards feel less pressure to cater to parental consumers because the cost of running for the board is high—so high, in fact, that in most cases, one cannot do it without the help of teachers' unions. And thus, the problem goes back to square one.

Even when an incompetent and educationally destructive teacher can be removed, it's rarely the end of the line. Far too frequently, bad teachers are simply reassigned to new schools where no one is familiar with them. Sometimes, teachers are so bad they get bounced around to several different schools in relatively short periods of times. So common is this in public schools that the education system even has its own nomenclature for this practice: "the Dance of the Lemons" and "the Turkey Trot." Who are the victims? School administrators, good teachers, and the teachers' unions know that nine times out of ten, the victims are minority children from low-income homes—those who need good teachers the most. The fact is minority and low-income parents are less likely to complain about bad teachers or wield the power needed to take on teachers' unions.

Once a teacher, no matter how bad, gets hired and gets union protection, the chances of getting rid of him or her is next to zero. One illuminating statistic comes from *The Incompetent Teacher: The Challenge and the Response* by Edwin M. Bridges. In California, 80 percent of all teachers are tenured; yet tenured teachers make up only 5 percent of those teachers who are fired. Temporary teachers make up 7 percent of the workforce, and yet they are 70 percent of the teachers who are dismissed.[23] And it's all because of the double whammy: uniform pay and union red tape—it means that teachers have no incentive, other than by their own consciences, to be competent, let alone succeed.

SUBSTITUTES FOR ACCOUNTABILITY

In the absence of financial incentives for better student performance, teachers are rewarded by an entirely counterproductive set of qualifications. According to union rules, the only acceptable reasons for increasing teachers' compensation are their seniority and the number of college courses completed.

In 1990, a history teacher at Fridley High School, Dr. Cathy Nelson, was named Minnesota's "Teacher of the Year." Ironically, at the time when this award was bestowed, Nelson was no longer teaching. She had already been laid off under a union bargained "last hired, first fired" policy. Though she had been a teacher for over fifteen years, she was the least senior of five history teachers at Fridley. This was the third time she had lost her job due to her lack of seniority. So at a time that should have been the pinnacle of her teaching career, a time when she should have been basking in compliments from the community and putting her award-winning methods to use on future generations, Nelson gave up teaching, the very same year she was recognized as the best in the state.[24]

It would have been very hard for Nelson to accrue any seniority if she kept getting fired for her lack of it. But this simply highlights the nonsensical nature of the current education system, which puts heavy financial priorities upon seniority and gives no salary bonuses to the best teachers. According to Bridges, bad teachers are "much more likely to appear among the most senior segment of the teaching force than the least senior."[25] Bridges attributes this to labor short-ages—when schools are desperate to fill a large number of positions, they are far less discriminating in who they hire because of a lack of available applicants. So they hire bad teachers, and once they are in the system and gain seniority, there's no firing them. However, it would be hard not to go a step further and suggest this correlation is also because some older teachers are painfully aware of how secure their jobs really are. The longer they teach, the harder they are to fire—so they stop making an effort at all. And for this, they are financially rewarded.

Of course, no matter what profession you are talking about, experience counts for something. This is why teachers' unions oppose accountability in our schools. They don't want the measures of achievement to even exist, for risk of identifying the best teachers and showing the public how unjust the system is. Teachers' unions and their emphasis on seniority have managed to find a way to conflate experience with excellence as a measure of worth. While the NEA actively fights any attempt to involuntarily assign teachers to subjects that are outside their area of expertise, it doesn't object to teachers *voluntarily* accepting such assignments. This is because when jobs are at stake, the unions protect the jobs of the most senior teachers by negotiating them into available positions within the district, regard-less of any expertise in the subject. Consequently, the Department of Education reports that a third of high school math teachers, a quar-ter of high school English teachers, and about a fifth of high school science teachers are teaching without either a major or minor in the subject area they are teaching.[26]

In the union mentality, no distinction exists between experience relevant to the particular subject someone teaches and simply get-ting your ticket punched. This also has a negative impact on teacher training, the other financial incentive for teacher improvement. Though teachers can increase their worth by going back to school and getting an advanced degree or other academic certification, it often doesn't matter if that degree relates only tangentially to their teaching job.

A few years ago, Barbara Kelley, the vice chair of the National Board for Professional Teaching Standards, told *U.S. News and World Report* that "salary is not what attracts people to teaching and keeps them there." Yet Kelley herself is a gym teacher from Maine who had just increased her salary substantially by earning an MBA. When pressed, she admitted to *U.S. News* that she was "thinking about leaving teaching and that the degree might help her in another career."[27]

This emphasis on continuing education, without regard for each individual teacher's specific professional development, only costs taxpayers money, and even encourages some to pursue opportunities to leave education. Thus, as the teachers' unions have shaped the system, a history major with a one-year teacher certificate and district tenure (given they have been in the district long enough to earn tenure) is more welcome in our education system than a chemical engineering doctorate who has retired and wants to teach to give back to the community.

So irrelevant is subject mastery and advanced education that teachers *cannot* be paid the highest salaries unless they get advanced degrees—*any* advanced degree. The Mackinac Center for Public Policy also points out that in their home state of Michigan, seniority alone will not allow teachers to rise to the top of the pay scale. Teachers with thirty years of experience, but who lack a master's or doctorate, will not max out the pay scale, regardless of their service or how effective they are as teachers.[28] This is also true in many other states. Thus, as teachers' unions have shaped the system, a fifteen-time "Teacher of the Year" in physics that spends several hours after school preparing illustrative lab demonstrations cannot be paid as much as a home economics major teaching with an MBA earned at night school.

Most scholars who have looked at these salary issues agree that neither seniority nor added credentials is any substitute for real accountability. As one scholar puts it, "Since teacher effectiveness generally declines after five years experience, and teacher credentials have been shown to be meaningless, the [disconnect] between service rendered and compensation received is all but complete."[29]

DISCOURAGING GOOD TEACHERS: NO ROOM FOR MAVERICKS

The remarkable thing about public education in this country is that even after all of these perverse and unjust incentives, some of our finest and most giving citizens are standing in front of a blackboard, trying to teach. This is where the real power of teachers' unions comes from. Most parents and taxpayers remember those one or two amazing teachers from their own experience and give, to any group with the name and self-proclaimed mission of protecting teachers, a measure of respect.

A great teacher is worth his or her weight in gold. Do you remember Jaime Escalante, hero of the film *Stand and Deliver*? Escalante's story is an amazing tale of success teaching calculus to barrio and inner city kids in Los Angeles. *Stand and Deliver* remains one of the most uplifting stories about human potential ever committed to film.

Escalante, a Bolivian immigrant, first gained national attention in 1982 when eighteen of his students passed the advanced placement (AP) exam for college credit in calculus. The school that Escalante taught at had been considered so poor and academically substandard that the Educational Testing Service (ETS) found the scores suspect and requested that fourteen of the eighteen students take the test again (the number of Hispanic students that passed the AP exam under Escalante's tutelage that year amounted to a third of Hispanic students that passed the test *nationwide*). Twelve of the fourteen students agreed to do it, despite howls of protests that they had earned their marks fair and square. All twelve passed the second time and their scores were reinstated.[30]

The incident garnered national attention and made Escalante something of a folk hero. Escalante expanded his program. The next year the number of Escalante's students that passed the exam doubled. By 1987, the number quadrupled, and by 1990, Escalante's math enrichment program involved over four hundred students; he and his fellow math teachers at Garfield High in Los Angeles referred to their program as "the dynasty."[31]

Unfortunately, the sequel to *Stand and Deliver* was never made. If it had been, the public would be outraged, because what happened to Escalante after the movie ends is a disgrace. If this story were widely known, it would be a public relations disaster for teachers' unions.

At the peak of his "dynasty," in 1990, Escalante wrote a letter to the union president about the atmosphere at his beloved Garfield High. "If you looked into what is going on in this school in the name of the union," he wrote, "I think you . . . would be appalled."[32]

What was going on? Escalante was under increasing pressure from union forces to stop doing what he was doing. He had made a career out of going around union strictures in the name of teaching his students. For years he got away with it because of administrative support and a reputation for success that was hard to argue with. In particular, a key element of Escalante's success was an open admission policy for his advanced math classes. Any student who wished to be taught advanced math simply had to ask. As a result, numerous students who would have normally been excluded from advanced placement courses were enrolled, and they succeeded convincingly. Many of Escalante's students went on to the nation's top universities. However, this resulted in large classes. Some had over 50 students, far beyond the union contract's rules, which mandated that no class be larger than 35. This was a major bone of contention.[33]

In 1991, Escalante finally got discouraged by the environment at

Garfield and left to teach in Sacramento. Several other math teachers in the program left too. When Escalante left, he put his dynasty in charge of a hand-picked successor, another Garfield math teacher named Angelo Villavicencio.

Without Escalante's formidable reputation to contend with, however, the union immediately began turning the screws on Villavicencio. First, Villavicencio had 107 calculus students and was denied permission to add a third Calculus section to get class sizes under 40. Then the new principal, Maria Elena Tostado, tried to take away the music hall from Villavicencio, which was the only classroom in the school large enough to accommodate more than 50 students.

That year, in spite of having lost a majority of the school's math teachers, Villavicencio still managed to get 47 students to pass the AP exam. But after a year in the face of obvious administrative hostility, Villavicencio wondered, "Am I going to have a heart attack defending the program?" He quit teaching at Garfield the following spring.[34] By 1996, in Escalante's absence, the dynasty had fallen apart. Only 11 students passed the AP exam, down from a high of 85.[35]

The class-size issue was just the final straw. To begin with, Escalante's dynasty was only made possible by copious amounts of union rule breaking. Ironically, when he taught his first class, there were only five students qualified to take it. Escalante had to bend the rules in order to teach a class that small. Still, it was this first small class that enabled Escalante to begin fulfilling his vision.[36]

The unsung hero of the Escalante story was Henry Gradillas, the principal at Garfield High for most of Escalante's career. Good teachers are like ace fighter pilots—some pilots are just clearly better than others. Since World War I, the armed services have fruitlessly dumped millions of dollars into determining why it is that some pilots stand head and shoulders above the rest. Aces are not necessarily the pilots with the best training or most preparation. Individually, they have very unique styles that often have little in common with other pilots.

But, when thrust into combat, the superior instincts and reflexes of an ace pilot immediately distinguish themselves, and it takes a superior officer to recognize this ability.

And so it is with teachers. Henry Gradillas immediately recognized that Escalante was more than simply a maverick teacher. He was the best there was. The Hollywood gloss over Escalante's story downplays the years of hard work Escalante put in to develop his renowned mathematics program. It took seven years of hard work creating the program before Escalante became nationally famous. During that time, Escalante worked hard to adequately prime some of the nation's most at-risk students for succeeding at advanced mathematics. He ratcheted up standards, created feeder programs at other schools, signed up other teachers to help him, and raised money. He even set up intensive seven-week summer courses in math for Garfield students at East Los Angeles College.

Early on, working outside the system in this manner earned Escalante a number of enemies. For example, an assistant principal tried to dismiss him for independently raising money, as well as for the grievous crimes of coming to school too early and keeping students too late! (If only this were a complaint with more teachers.) When problems like this arose, and they frequently did, Gradillas interceded and backed Escalante with his administrative authority in nearly every case. Even as complaints arose about the difficulty of the new higher standards, Gradillas didn't just stand firm, he raised the ante. He helped Escalante's program by instituting a new standard requiring all students taking basic math to also be concurrently taking Algebra. Gradillas also denied extracurricular activities to students who failed to maintain a C average.

Did the community rebel against these tough standards? Did the school fall apart under Escalante and Gradillas's challenge to their students? No, they succeeded spectacularly—even surpassing their own expectations. In the beginning, Gradillas stated publicly that he hoped that the math program at Garfield High in East Los Angeles would come close to equaling the success of the Beverly Hills High School, which had seemingly limitless resources. In 1987, Gradillas's last year at Garfield, it did.[37]

Unfortunately, that was also the year that Gradillas took a year-long sabbatical to finish his doctorate. He had hoped to regain his job as principal at Garfield, or be given a position where he could help replicate programs like Escalante's at other schools. But despite his overwhelming success, Gradillas hadn't played by union rules. So upon his return, he was given a plum position supervising asbestos removal.[38] From that point on, Escalante's administrative support was slowly undermined, eventually leading to his departure four years later.

The moral of the story here is that teachers who succeed spectacularly, like Escalante, should be held up as an example to raise the bar and challenge their professional peers to achieve higher standards.

But as it stands now, union rules are set up to drag teachers like Escalante down to the lowest common denominator, not the other way around. Union contracts demand the absolute minimum of effort from teachers. For instance, it is possible in New York to be a teacher at the top of the pay scale, working about twenty-eight hours a week, thirty-six weeks a year, under an unbelievably comprehensive contract that forbids them from doing things such as "attending more than one staff meeting per month after school hours, walking the children to a school bus, patrolling the hallways or the lunchroom or the schoolyard, covering an extra class in an emergency, attending a lunchtime staff meeting, or coming in a few days prior to the opening of school each September to do some planning."[39] In fact, New York's teacher's contract even stipulates "'the school day . . . shall be 6 hours and 20 minutes' and that the school year lasts from the Tuesday after Labor Day until June 26. School principals may not require teachers to be in the building one day before that Tuesday, one minute before the students arrive each day, or one minute after the students leave."[40]

Though many unsung teachers make the effort, we know many slide by on the absolute minimum in these circumstances. The continued existence of teachers like Escalante, who succeed by innovation and by going the extra mile for the benefit of students, exposes the farce of teachers' union contracts that would protect lazy and incompetent teachers, by telling everyone what they can or cannot do. Escalante achieved the educational equivalent of putting a man on the moon because he believed in himself, believed in his students, and worked damn hard. That teachers' unions would get in the way of hardworking and successful teachers by constructing and enforcing unnecessarily elaborate contracts, I believe, is almost a manifestation of guilt—to legitimize their failings with the illegitimate absolution of legal protection.

Certainly not every teacher can be as successful as Escalante. But to judge him by contractual union standards and deny his success as a rogue teacher, rather than an extraordinary example, is a crime. Escalante succeeded because he demanded more from his students at every turn. And we should let his success lead by example. All teachers can succeed if they try, but only if we—as parents, politicians, school board members, and administrators—demand more from them and hold our ground. Not every teacher will prove as extraordinary as Escalante. But every teacher can still work hard and achieve for his or her students if we demand it. And when that happens, the nation should pay them handsomely, in terms of both respect and financial reward.

5

A SEAT AT BOTH SIDES
OF THE NEGOTIATING TABLE

During the late 1980s, and throughout the 1990s, the Los Angeles Unified School District (LAUSD) faced more challenges than most other districts. It is the second largest school district in the nation, with more than seven hundred thousand students who speak 152 different languages and come from all kinds of different backgrounds. And, because of its size, the LAUSD's responsibility to the public is awesome—almost the entire generation of future Los Angelenos depends on the stewardship of that body.

However, several years ago it had become apparent that the LAUSD had failed utterly in this task of stewarding these seven hundred thousand children. In 1999, things had become so bad that the *Daily News of Los Angeles* editorialized, "For two decades, LAUSD's board and administrative leadership have promoted failure, rewarded ideology over excellence and pushed achievement to the back of the bus."[1] How did this sorry state of affairs come about? "Unions received everything. Children, if they were lucky, got the budget leftovers."[2]

Despite a whopping $7 billion budget, over a third of LAUSD's students failed to graduate—twice the state average. For those who did graduate, with dismal SAT scores and abysmal literacy rates among grade school students (thanks largely to failed bilingual programs), diplomas meant little more than "Congratulations, you sat in your seat and fulfilled your seat time requirement." Functionally, that diploma was worth nothing more than the paper it was printed on. The Los Angeles education system had little more to show for itself than high dropout rates, illiteracy, and remedial education.

Mayor Richard Riordan, a successful businessman who had already proven he had a heart for educating LA students, saw the appalling tragedy of this state of affairs. While board meetings went late into the night, as member Victoria Castro argued about who got to speak next, and member Barbara Boudreaux fought to get Ebonics taught in the classroom, Mayor Riordan seized the initiative to reform and willingly confronted the brutal facts.

And the mayor did not mince words. Riordan called the system "evil [and] criminal" for its failure to educate children. He added, "The number one crime in Los Angeles and California today is our education system."[3] In response to the appalling state of affairs and in defiance of the status quo's acceptance of failure, Mayor Riordan sought to turn frustration into action: "We need to find people who are willing to put children ahead of politics. The only policy we should have is what is best for our children."[4]

I respect Riordan greatly for his stance; he was one of the earliest of the business reformers, and the first to take on a big city education system by appealing directly to the public. He risked a great deal because, compared to other mayors, the mayor of Los Angeles does not wield much power over the schools. His influence was limited to directing his calls to the public. As a private citizen, Riordan worked to provide more resources, fund-raising, and new computers for the schools—exactly what guardians of the status quo wanted. Once he became mayor, he was set to take on those in control, and he knew the power of the ground troops being commanded by teachers' unions and other special interests in education. His failure should be an object lesson for all those who cling to the belief that teachers' unions care about children and not about political power.

Riordan's first move was to gather a coalition to fight for the needs of children, against the teachers' unions. He supported and organized a slate of candidates to take on the incumbents of the LAUSD board. Unfortunately, like many who attempt to reform their local school board, Riordan didn't necessarily know that he also set out to target the teachers' unions. Teachers' unions use their considerable clout to ensure that an overwhelming number of the candidates they support get elected to the school board. The very same people elected to allegedly represent the educational and financial interests of the community against the teachers' unions are, in fact, often politically backed by the union to support union goals.

It's a disappointing reality that almost all systemic school board reforms are met with union opposition. Many school boards around the country traffic almost exclusively in union affairs. Collective bargaining agreements can take years to hammer out, even in small districts. The handful of parents and citizens who have nobly asked for the privilege of sacrificing nearly all of their free time for a demanding, thankless, and prestige-free job frequently find themselves overwhelmed by the unions' army of full-time organizers and legal experts.

Unfortunately, stories like this one play out all over the nation. Districts where school boards stand up to teachers' unions are the battlegrounds for some of the most bitter and divisive politics in the nation. They are so divisive that the most high-profile politicians avoid these conflicts as much as possible, for fear that they will bring their entire political career to an end. So, it is all the more remarkable that Riordan dove into the fray, headfirst. The LAUSD was so big and politicized, and the unions had so much at stake, that many observers thought Riordan might be sending his political career down the tubes.

When board member George Kiriyama heard about Riordan's plan, his response showed just how insular, unaccountable, and removed the board had become. He didn't voice any concern about children; he didn't address the abysmal failures of the system; he didn't take up the gauntlet challenging the board's responsibilities. Instead, he got lost in minutiae and complained that the mayor did not bring his complaints to board members "personally." In fact, his disconnect from the reality of poor student achievement and his focus on his own job security bordered on the surreal: "I would like to know why [Riordan] is opposing me personally and what [it] is that I am not doing."[5]

Here was the unions' handpicked candidate, so isolated from accountability and the need to educate real, live students that he was unable to fathom why it might bother citizens that children weren't learning and the system was broken. But even in the face of imminent threat, teachers' unions and their candidates could not acknowledge the truth. The famous definition of a fanatic is a person who fails utterly, but then still redoubles his efforts. So, too, do teachers' unions. The United Teachers-Los Angeles (UTLA) president showed in microcosm the hardheadedness and arrogance facing reformers who are trying to improve public schools for our children. UTLA's president Day Higuchi said of this relentless battery of school board candidates, "If God himself ran a candidate against them, we'd defend them."[6]

For Los Angeles, the ugly campaign politics were just about to begin. And as always, the first impulse of those supporting the status quo is to get personal and impugn motives. But in this case, such an attack was hard to make. Riordan wasn't trying to increase his power. He had little to gain personally. Any improvements in education would be felt long after he left office. In addition, the accountability he sought was in creating a board that would give the LAUSD superintendent of schools more power to ensure accountability. He simply wanted to keep the board from intruding in operations and focus on performance, achievement, and results.

While the objectors of school reform could not grasp this, the public did. As the *Daily News of Los Angeles* editorial board wrote:

> As it stands today, the Board of Education answers to everyone except the people who matter most: parents, children, taxpayers. The district needs tough love to survive. That means firing principals who don't lead. Firing teachers who can't do the job. Cleaning house of the hundreds of cronies, relatives and just plain stupid bureaucrats who rob children blind. If a movement claiming to be "for the children" is to be believed and is genuine, it must put students first. The priority must be on creating a curriculum that works, instructing teachers to use it, measuring progress through testing and holding students, teachers, principals, schools and the district accountable.[7]

Riordan spoke as a businessman who understood how organizations define themselves: "If you're a principal and you know the superintendent doesn't have any authority over you, you're not going to listen to him."[8]

As a former superintendent, I have a hard time understanding exactly why anyone could object to giving the superintendent such authority. No sane shareholder would ever demand a CEO to clean up the books, turn around the company, and improve the product without giving him the authority to hire and fire.

In fact, this hire-fire authority is more important for improving traditional public schools precisely because the system is a monopoly. In the consumer-oriented arena of the private sector, a bad manager or employee can only last so long before people turn to other companies to meet their needs. If we are to continue with the monopolistic, zero-choice structure of education, parents need the assurance that the incompetent, corrupt, and criminal school officials will be removed. The cost is simply too high to demand parents to let their children suffer.

Likewise, how can a superintendent communicate the right ideas and reward the best teachers and principals without being able to reward those teachers who put in the extra hours, give their instruction that extra polish, and inspire children with new ideas?

When this kind of accountability and authority is lacking from the superintendent, the result is inevitable: school boards get lost in minutiae. It's no wonder that LAUSD school board meetings went past midnight meeting after meeting after meeting.

For instance, Mike Lansing, who was later inspired to challenge an incumbent board member, pointed out:

> Two weeks in a row, I saw the same two nice girls come up and complain that their restrooms weren't open, and then the superintendent says, "Yes, we're going to look into this"—and this was about a 20-minute discussion on why these restrooms were being closed. . . . I asked myself, why is that being discussed at a school board meeting?[9]

A school board, mind you, that spends more than $7 billion a year.[10] In other meetings, the board members debated about what schools would serve for lunch and hosted particularly nasty fights about teaching Ebonics. Locked in such ridiculous and chaotic discussions, it should be no surprise that board members voted to build a $200 million state-of-the-art Belmont Learning Complex on toxic land.[11] When it wasn't a debate about trivial items, it was just debate.

Here is a reprint of one of those altercations: a debate about whether school police should be allowed to carry shotguns in emergencies. As the *Los Angeles Times* noted when it reprinted this LAUSD board transcript, "Coherence and civility are parts of good governance. That lesson needs to be learned by some members of the Los Angeles school board."[12]

Barbara Boudreaux: . . . I know guns. I know how deadly guns can be. I do not have guns around my children, my grandchildren. My husband when he found out I could shoot over 45 years ago . . . he decided no guns in the house for Barbara Boudreaux because he figured I would not miss . . .

Valerie Fields: Ms. Boudreaux, I'm sure you didn't mean to say that you had a shotgun wedding. I know that's not true.

Boudreaux: No, not a shotgun wedding. No, in our family we wait at least not nine months but more than nine months before we got pregnant, but I know how to use a shotgun.

Fields: May I start my time over? May I start my time? . . . Ms. Castro's dream could turn into a nightmare, if we have kids locked down in an auditorium and there's a shotgun brought onto campus because there's an incident and one kid's been in the bathroom and runs.

Victoria Castro: My experience has been the opposite.

Fields: Excuse me! Excuse me. . . .

Castro: Well, since you made reference to me . . .

Fields: Excuse me! Excuse me. . . .

Julie Korenstein, president of the board: Let her finish.

Fields: Excuse me for talking. . . .

Castro: My dream . . . (unintelligible as board members talked over each other) turned into misery. . . .

Boudreaux: Don't use your time to attack other board members, just . . .

Fields: I'm not. I'm asking a question. I did not interrupt you, and I don't expect to be interrupted. . . .

Castro: Well, I didn't make reference to you either.

Korenstein: Let her finish.

Fields: May I have my time extended? . . .

Castro: My experiences are obviously very different from yours.

Korenstein: Go on. Go on. Go on.

Fields: Ms. Castro, excuse me for talking while you're interrupting.

Korenstein: Go on. Go on. You have a minute left, so please go ahead.

Fields: Your dream could turn into a nightmare, if a child were killed by a shotgun. . . .

Castro: And I've been there when a child's been killed.

Fields: Excuse me! This is my time.

Korenstein: Go ahead, Valerie.

Castro: Well excuse me, if you continue to make me be used as a reference . . .

Korenstein: All right.

Castro: I want to give you clarity.

Fields: Why don't you give it to me on your time?

Castro: I don't understand what your beliefs are of my experiences.

Fields: Why don't you give it to me on your time?

Castro: But I have been there when a student has been shot.

Korenstein: All right.

Castro: And a student has been killed. . . .

Korenstein: Vicki . . .

Castro: So I don't live in La-La Land.

Korenstein: Vicki, let me provide you another time, another round to respond.

Fields: Yes. That seems to me the polite way to do business.

David Tokofsky: If necessary, could the chair use the gavel?

Fields: I can imagine a situation where the kids are all locked down, they are in the auditorium except for one kid who is in the bathroom. . . .

Korenstein: I need a shotgun, that's what I need.

Fields: . . . Who runs out just as a shotgun is fired and the broadcast can hit that kid. It's just as possible. I don't think any of us would want to experience that because it would be our fault because we allowed the shotguns to be deployed. That would give me nightmares, and I don't think I could ever overcome that. Today, there was a march to restore the dream, Ms. Boudreaux. . . .

Boudreaux: Yes, I walked it, but you didn't.

Fields: Excuse me, please.

Korenstein: Let her finish, please. You only have a few seconds left.

Fields: I would like to have marched in that, too. But Martin Luther King, whose dream it was, was a man of nonviolence, and certainly did not talk about rearming or arming people. He was a pacifist. That's all I have to say.[13]

Unfortunately, this kind of ridiculous, time-wasting dialogue is replayed day after day in school board meetings across the nation. The parents, business leaders, and public are not just excluded from education reform by the teachers' unions' money and those who oppose school reform's contempt for outside influence. The American people are locked out by almost equally formidable obstacles: bullying and bureaucratic bigotry. Parents who attend school board meetings to talk about real problems or to demand real measures of performance rarely find them—even when important discussions are made public. Teachers' unions support 80 to 90 percent of winning school board candidates.[14] And the politically partisan teachers' union leadership abhors accountability and results-oriented school board members.

LAUSD is just one well-documented example of common complaints and experiences. But this lack of focus is rarely seen. Few newspapers make education a priority assignment for journalists, and even fewer editorial boards make a point of tracking their local school boards as assiduously as the writers and reporters in Los Angeles did. Before No Child Left Behind and the national debate about accountability, many newspapers simply lacked access to the numbers and evidence to credibly follow what was going on in local schools. That has begun to change. But the public needs to see how boards like LAUSD's really work—who they really support and how little regard they have for children falling behind.

As I crisscrossed America in my four years as secretary, I heard from concerned parents from all over the nation and from every kind of background. I heard from good-hearted business leaders. And listened to fed-up teachers and disillusioned principals who needed support from local school districts but weren't getting it. To say the least, it was dishonest.

Consider for a moment what the transcript quoted above really means. Without a singular and unwavering focus on the mission of public education, the trivial and unimportant matters dominate those that are important and urgent. And the guardians of mediocrity don't know what to do, because they oppose measures of progress—conducting testing, implementing standards, and demanding results. So, while seven hundred thousand children were getting some of the worst schooling in the country, the LAUSD's school board was lost. Instead of trying to increase accountability and give the superintendent and principals more authority to meet higher expectations, board members voted themselves $30,000 to spend on group therapy so they could get along better. This gall prompted the *Daily News of Los Angeles* to opine, "Los Angeles doesn't need its school board to attend group therapy sessions; it needs a new group."[15]

As former LA superintendent of schools Ruben Zacarias said, "I'm not interested in training that teaches them to be nicer to each other. I'm interested in training that will clearly define their roles, responsibilities and limits as [policymakers], not implementers."[16]

No therapist, however gifted, could bring these members together. But one thing could: the threat that they might lose their jobs. In fact, that $30,000 for therapy pales in comparison to the brazen behavior of the school board in the face of Riordan's reform efforts. Knowing they were in trouble, the board turned to the teachers' and public employees' unions who had picked, funded, and gotten them elected in the first place. In an example of the worst kind of Machiavellianism, the teachers' unions blatantly used the mayor's efforts to help children to further line their own wallets.

In the face of voter accountability, the LAUSD board members chose to direct an additional $54 million to give teachers pay raises that year.[17] What's amazing is that these 2 percent pay raises came in the middle of a settled, signed, and already established contract. One year earlier, the district had negotiated a 10 percent pay raise over three years; but now, here was the board reopening the contract to pay teachers, and through compulsory dues collection, teachers' unions, more. It was obviously an effort to pay off the masters who were needed to defend their lackeys. But more importantly, it was a measure of the lack of accountability in education, and clear exemplification of the difficulty of electing school members who are not controlled by teachers' unions, that these members were willing to risk public condemnation instead of trying to raise performance for the sake of pupils.

The school board members, hand-picked by the teachers' unions, saw no reason to focus on the welfare of students or on such troublesome matters as results. One of my fundamental Maxims of American Education (see appendix A) dictates that you don't need to know anything about a school's test results or a district's assessments to know whether kids are doing well. You can tell simply by listening to principals, teachers, and board members. They either believe that kids can learn or they do not. If they do not believe all children can learn, all you'll hear are excuses—why they need more money, fewer demands, and more teachers. So it was with these pitiful unions' candidates in the City of Angels. For them, this intolerable failure dooming kids year after year was how the system was supposed to work.

The *Los Angeles Times* asked candidates whether the Los Angeles Unified School District was in crisis. The answers were shocking:

Incumbent Barbara Boudreaux: "Not really, not in crisis. I think [LAUSD] is working toward growing up, and when you begin to start growing up, and I'm willing to give that support with others to make it grow up, I don't think it's in total crisis."[18]

Brutal Fact: More than two out of three students could not read at grade level by the end of third grade.[19]

Incumbent Jeff Horton: "Performance has not been that disastrous."[20]

Brutal Fact: Math and reading scores ranked in the bottom third in the nation.[21]

Incumbent George Kiriyama: "Well, I don't know."[22]

Brutal Fact: Sixty-seven percent of white parents graded their local public schools as fair to poor. Nearly 70 percent of black parents handed out a similar failing grade. And 56 percent of Latino parents agreed.[23] Strong majorities of black and white parents (and 44 percent of Latino parents) said they would send their children to private or parochial schools if they could.[24] Citizens gave the Los Angeles Police Department a much higher approval rating than the schools—this despite Rodney King and a number of high-profile corruption scandals throughout the 90s.[25]

Only one incumbent, David Tokofsky, seemed to understand that the district needed serious reform because it was in dire straits. He gave an answer that mirrored what many parents thought: "Yes [the district is in crisis]. My daughter's 7 months old, and if I'm elected again, it's during that term that I will decide whether she goes to kindergarten in L.A. Unified or not."[26]

Brutal Fact: At least he was honest. Twenty-five percent of teachers vote with their feet, choosing to send their own children to private schools instead of to the public schools at which they teach.[27]

In contrast to this whistle-past-the-graveyard mentality, Riordan's candidates saw the imperative of immediate and resolute action. They were willing to confront the ugly, brutal facts of widespread failure. Abysmal performance and lost dreams were not something to explain away. They were a spur to immediate reform and decisive action.

Boudreaux's challenger, Genethia Hayes, stated unequivocally, "Absolutely [the district is in crisis]. And it needs triage work. . . . Those of us who are looking for seats on the board have to hit the ground running in being able to say that the district is in crisis."[28]

Caprice Young, the challenger for Jeff Horton's job, was also unequivocal about the crisis: "I think the number one reason why the district is in the mess that it's in is that, for the last 15 years, parents and business, then significant numbers of people, have given up and not participated. I think that has meant that the unions' and the people who are impacted everyday—teachers, predominately, and the different employee unions—have really run the district."[29]

Young's ideas were designed to inject new life into the district. Not only did she recognize the crisis and the teachers' unions' disconnect from reality, she clearly identified places for reform. She added, "I don't think people on the board really, fully comprehend the depth of the crisis that we have in getting enough qualified teachers into the schools."[30] She put her finger on a problem those of us in the Bush administration would try to tackle seven years later—there were not enough good, high-quality teachers. Twenty-five percent of LAUSD teachers were on emergency credentials; in other words, they lacked teaching credentials but had been hired to fill vacancies. Young called this state of affairs a "major crisis."[31]

Young's position wasn't just idle talk. She planned on using the Committee on Effective School Governance report to set sixty-day goals, hire an inspector general, and implement phonics as a classroom reading tool. She even raised the stakes for success, saying the board should get two years to fix major problems or face real accountability—the dissolution of the district into smaller parts.[32]

The teachers' unions and their incumbent lackeys were considered so out of touch and their opponents so earnest and energetic that the liberal *Los Angeles Times* backed the reformers. The *LA Times* editorial says a lot about the crisis:

> The Los Angeles school district is running out of time. The nation's second largest district has many excellent teachers and numerous students who win academic awards, but their achievements occur in spite of an inept system that doesn't give them the proper materials, financial support or educational direction. The public is losing patience with endless excuses for why two-thirds of third-graders fail to read at grade level. The problems extend through all grades. Parents are frustrated with the plodding pace of progress represented by last year's gain of two percentile points in reading and math scores. At that rate, the majority of students will fail each year for the next 10 years.[33]

Nearly every voice, except the teachers' unions, joined in this chorus of warning and concern. In February 1999, an eighteen-member task force assembled by then superintendent Ruben Zacarias—a man so dependent on the whims and wishes of the board—concluded:

> The way the LAUSD board conducts the district's affairs is a reason our students receive a substandard education. . . . The board practices undermine the authority of the superintendent, principals, teachers; cause confusion and needless disputes about how to use money and lead to great inefficiency and, often, to unfairness.[34]

DIRTY POLITICS

One of the great tragedies of American education is that this kind of united resolve and concern for public school performance is rare. More than 90 percent of all public school funding comes from state and local sources. But awareness is low and knowledge incomplete about how local schools are performing (or more than often failing to perform). Here in LAUSD, for a moment, the public, business leaders, journalists, and a courageous mayor united against the formidable might of the teachers' unions and their establishment lackeys.

Their failure in the face of overwhelming union power helped expose why the nation needed presidential leadership and the No Child Left Behind Act. Teachers' unions were driven by perverse incentives that put them in opposition to reform; and their self-interest led them to oppose any outside influence not purchased by the compulsory dues taken from classroom teachers, those working on the frontlines of education.

THE EMPIRE STRIKES BACK

On Election Day, 13 April 1999, Mayor Richard Riordan's hard work paid off, but just barely. It was a measure of the financial strength and political heft of teachers' unions that only one challenger had a clear lead the following day: challenger Caprice Young. Challenger Mike Lansing and Riordan-backed incumbent David Tokofsky pulled out close wins. A few months later, challenger Genethia Hayes would win her run-off election against the embarrassing incumbent, Barbara Boudreaux.

As the *Los Angeles Times* declared after the election, "The results reflect an amazing successful uprising against two incumbents who were tied to poor test scores, poor management and poor excuses."[35]

For almost any big city school district, the story of LAUSD's board is a morality play. It is a reminder of what reformers face and, more importantly, the incredible lust for power that drives teachers' unions and other groups against school reform.

The new LAUSD board began to institute real reforms, the simple, common sense ideas such as higher standards, taxpayer-friendly audits, and greater support for principals. Things started improving immediately. Once again my fundamental Maxim of American Education (see appendix A) was proven correct: all children can learn. In just four years after Riordan organized his successful campaign to elect new and responsible school board members, grade-school math and reading scores *doubled*. And this happened even at poor schools packed with immigrants—schools that the LA teachers' union had, for years, been blaming for dragging down the average scores. Even Jill Stewart, a columnist at the *Daily News of Los Angeles* who had generated many column inches over the board's numerous failings, concluded that the city should be "throwing a ticker tape parade for Caprice Young, David Tokofsky and the board."[36]

But did anyone throw Hayes, Tokofsky, or Young a parade? Absolutely not. Despite their astounding success since taking office as part of Riordan's reform movement, the board members and the teachers' union had targets on their back from day one. When they came up for reelection in 2003, Riordan's reformers Caprice Young and Genethia Hayes were defeated; Tokofsky barely hung on to his seat. This was something that Jill Stewart had rightly noted could only come about as a result of "sheer ignorance."[37]

Of course, that level of ignorance rarely comes out in the electorate naturally. It has to be bought and paid for; and the teachers' unions pay handsomely for it. The United Teachers-Los Angeles (UTLA) offered a large portion of the nearly $2 million spent during the race against Caprice Young to any candidate who wished to oppose her in the election.[38] Three different recruits turned the UTLA down once they realized how much of the union's bidding would be required of them. After examining lists of failed office seekers, the union finally found a candidate in Jon Lauritzen, a former teacher.[39]

Lauritzen succeeded in defeating Young, largely because of an absolutely mendacious campaign ad that accused Young of spending

$100,000 on her private bathroom in the LAUSD headquarters.[40] Caprice Young was a mother of three who drove a used car and gave up a salary as an IBM executive to take the $24,000-a-year job on the school board. To have an also-ran like Lauritzen accuse Young of this kind of impropriety was the height of arrogance.

But doing the right thing and supporting effective school board members was the furthest concern for teachers' unions, who simply wanted someone on the board to do their bidding. They were all too happy to spend millions of dollars and engage in dirty politics. Perhaps one of the most damaging things about the union's spending was what had become known as the "Riordan Revolution"—the way that the union engaged in class warfare during the campaign. In the process of accusing Riordan of impropriety, one campaign worker for a union-backed candidate told the *LA Weekly* that he didn't want to give his name; he said, "I don't have enough power to confront Mr. Riordan. I am not white. It wouldn't take much to make me homeless."[41]

Even the *LA Weekly*, a publication that recently had the audacity to put a picture of President George W. Bush on the cover as the devil, had trouble swallowing that, saying that this sentiment was "an ironic fit on men who've invested time, money and prestige into bettering the city—unlike much of the city's disengaged wealthy, who dither or cower within their gate-guarded enclaves."[42] So, pillars of the community, take note. If you are considering the clearly crazy idea of putting your own money and efforts into improving the local schools, beware. Not only will your efforts go unrewarded, but despite spectacular successes, the teachers' unions will also attempt to portray you in the local media as a racist scrooge who delights in sending families out of their homes and onto the streets.

But what is so pernicious about this particular mind-set is that it is a key component of the cycle that allows unions to continue to justify failure in inner city schools. For years, the union and the school board in Los Angeles have been blaming their failure to educate on poverty rather than examining their own practices or holding themselves accountable. Of course, the worse the schools got, the more the middle class fled the city for better schools in the suburbs. The dwindling middle class heightened the poverty inside the city, resulting in a kind of self-fulfilling prophecy.

The Riordan Revolution completely shattered that myth, depriving teachers' unions of that precious excuse. Students could be educated in a fiscally responsible way, despite huge obstacles like widespread poverty and immigration. That this was proven by a rich and powerful businessman such as Riordan, with no practical expertise in education, just added insult to injury.

As it stands now, some eight years after the beginning of the Riordan Revolution, despite some successes, the people in Los Angeles are still as frustrated as ever about the condition of their schools. Bob Hertzberg, a Democratic candidate for mayor in 2005, said that his first priority as mayor would be to break up the LAUSD into a handful of smaller districts with more local oversight.[43] The UTLA was terrified of this and did everything they could to make sure it didn't happen.

Unfortunately the struggles in Los Angeles are more representative of school board politics than not. That the unions would cause this much unnecessary havoc is no surprise; even in small districts, collective bargaining agreements can take upward of five years to resolve. The unions have the power and resources to eventually overwhelm even the most powerful coalitions like Riordan's.

The unions will stop at nothing until they occupy both sides of the negotiation table. But more and more powerful politicians and community members are finding it hard to ignore this perversion of educational interests. More opposition to teachers' union assaults on democratic school boards is likely to emerge in the future, despite the feelings of futility that Riordan's defeat might encourage. Riordan himself had gone on to become California's own education secretary, under Governor Schwarzenegger, and was busy institutionalizing the lessons of his fight for the soul of the LAUSD. To quote the *LA Weekly*, "The reformers are dead. Long live the reformers."[44]

If all this just seems like a distant memory, it isn't. The LAUSD school board election coup represented an early major battle for school reform by those wishing to work within the system by raising accountability and responsiveness. Nearly any reform, no matter how moderate or commonsensical, must be opposed by union special interests. And, as if that weren't enough, San Diego's schools showed the nation once again the challenges of saving public education from the union leaders who control it.

By 1998, it was widely perceived that the local teachers' union was essentially running the school system in San Diego and had far too much influence over almost every operational detail. That's when members of the community started mobilizing to bring in a superintendent who could get the situation under control. They invited the local NEA chapter, the San Diego Education Association (SDEA), to participate in the selection process; but ultimately, against the union's wishes, they selected Alan Bersin, a former US attorney for Southern California, as the new superintendent.

Bersin had been brought in by local business and community leaders to run the school district after years of frustration with weak district leadership. A five-day strike by the SDEA in 1996 had led to a number of major capitulations to the union, as well as public embarrassment. Meanwhile, student performance was still lagging.

From the beginning, the SDEA perceived Bersin as illegitimate because his selection was the first major decision, since the strike, not more or less dictated by the union. The other major criticism was that Bersin was not an educator. He was, however, a lawyer, and considering that the most recent problems that the San Diego School District faced were contractual matters, it should have sent a message.

Bersin was also a competent manager and, as such, recognized his shortcomings in the education arena. To combat this perception regarding his lack of educational experience, he almost immediately hired Anthony Alvarado—a school administrator who had received national recognition for turning New York City's Community School District 2 into a model of how an urban school district could be reformed and improved. While other school districts in California were beginning to embrace inevitable education reforms, "San Diego Unified was absolutely in a cocoon."[45]

Rather than waiting around, Bersin and Alvarado drew up a blueprint for reform, based heavily on two priorities. Their priorities were one, improving literacy by mandating as much as three hours a day of instruction on the subject in classrooms, and two, improving teacher performance in the classroom by putting peer coaches and consultants in classrooms to improve the teachers' professional ability. Alvarado had worked successfully with this plan before, and it was designed to have an immediate impact.[46]

Alvarado and Bersin did what few school administrators have the guts to do—they took the initiative, formed a sound plan, and acted on it without dithering. They should have been commended.

Instead, all hell broke loose.

"Like two scorpions in battle"—that's how observers described the relationship between San Diego School superintendent Alan Bersin and Marc Knapp, union president of the San Diego Education Association (SDEA).[47] In January 2003, California Teachers Association president Wayne Johnson gave Bersin a handwritten note that read, "I think you are the worst thing to happen to public education that I know of. I think you are one of the biggest jerks I have ever met. I stand behind everything I have ever said or written about you."[48] In 2002, as Bersin gave his annual State of the District speech, protesters marched outside the building; one carried a sign comparing Bersin to a Nazi.[49] This is what happens when you try and reform a school district against union wishes. It ain't pretty.

Despite achieving a great deal of success, Bersin never got as far as he should have for someone with his initiative and goals. The union fought him every step of the way, and even went so far as to make vicious personal attacks, as explained above.

While Bersin and Alvarado are both New Yorkers with hard-charging personalities, the fact that union organizers were constantly whining about these men being "abrasive" and difficult to work with was hardly cause for concern. That tells me that they were doing something right for a change. A union organizer calling a superintendent abrasive! Talk about the pot and kettle. What the ranks of school reformers need right now are top-down, take-no-prisoners leaders like Bersin and Alvarado.

Unfortunately, the major obstacles standing in the way of reform, and the teachers' unions' main weapon, are teachers' union contracts. It would be one thing if these contracts provided basic employee rights and protections; but, over the years these contracts have institutionalized teacher control to the point where even the most brazen and daring reformers, such as Bersin and Alvarado, cannot get very far.

Alvarado's pet project was putting peer coaches in the classroom—where the administration identifies the most successful teachers and uses them to coach teachers who need a little help. He had worked quite successfully with this program in the past, and it was the perfect opportunity for the union to get involved and participate in a real, educational improvement plan.

Instead the union balked, claiming that the program would turn teachers into "snitches" against underperforming teachers. The union also wanted to essentially neuter the program by controlling the selection of coaches, by making union reps and teachers at each individual school responsible for selecting the coaches. Teachers choosing their own peer coaches, rather than upper management selecting coaches based on their actual ability and performance in the classroom, would defeat the purpose.

The dispute over this program eventually boiled over into bitter third-party negotiations. Ultimately, the teachers' contractual say over staff development won out. Another good reform idea bit the dust.

The other problem encountered by Bersin was simply one of institutional inertia; it's a good example of how disrespectful the unions are of governmental authority.

The SDEA didn't like Bersin from the get-go. He wasn't their pick for the position; they regarded him as illegitimate, even though they had no sanctioned governmental authority to hire anyone to lead the district. They were privileged to even participate in the discussion about hiring, but that's never how unions view it. They're even outright disrespectful of the democratic wishes of the community. Compounding the problem for the union was the fact that Bersin had a majority of the elected school board supporting him. *Their* elections were far from illegitimate.

Instead of respecting the representatives of the community, or even acknowledging their success, unions simply dig their heels in and wait to get new representatives. After all, the vast majority of winning candidates have union money and support—as we saw in the LAUSD conflict, even the most effective school board members are vulnerable without union backing. But Bersin was lucky; in 2002, the SDEA unsuccessfully spent over $600,000 on campaigns to elect school board members not aligned with Bersin.[50]

The unions can afford to show such arrogance in the face of elected officials due to the power of their contracts. Because of all of the protections afforded to unions and teachers through contracts, only so much can be changed in a set period of time. It's not unheard of for contract negotiations to go as long as five years, even in local school districts. During that time, several board members may be up for reelection. Therefore, each election represents another opportunity to make the climate for the unions more favorable.

So, rather than respecting Bersin's authority, the SDEA simply decided to wait it out. In the meantime, they filed one petty grievance after another, even for the most minor procedural issues, for no other reason than to make the superintendent look bad, hoping that they could sully him in such a way as to influence the next school board decision.

While Bersin was remarkably successful in avoiding this trap, many well-intentioned administrators and school board members aren't so lucky. Public accountability and elections make them vulnerable to union tactics; meanwhile, unions are girded with a remarkable degree of contractual protection.

Like the LAUSD conflict, the story of Bersin shows that a lot can be accomplished in school reform. Unlike the LAUSD conflict, the Bersin story shows how some progress can be made without being immediately stomped on by a vengeful union.

And yet, nowhere in either story is there any hope that necessary reforms can occur unless the imbalance in contractual negotiations is realigned and shifted away from the unions. The authority should rest squarely on public officials and elected school board members— who actually do bow to the altar of accountability, and don't hide behind lawyers and mountains of contractual armor.

This does a tremendous amount of damage to the educational system. The Pacific Research Institute did a study on the impact of collective bargaining in California school districts. The results don't inspire much hope, but they do point the way to some obvious reforms:

- California's ten largest school districts have the most restrictive contracts—including Oakland, Sacramento, Los Angeles, San Diego, San Francisco, San Bernardino, Fresno, Orange, Santa Ana, and San Juan.
- In an average California school district, *85 percent of the district's operating budget is tied to teacher and employee salaries and collective bargaining contracts.* Districts with the most

restrictive clauses regarding school and classroom management spend a much higher percentage of their budget on salaries and benefits.

- Districts with no teacher contracts or union representation score higher on the state's student assessment test (SAT-9). Teachers in these districts also reported high satisfaction with district management.
- Districts with the most favorable scores and most flexible contracts are located almost entirely in northern and central California. Districts with smaller enrollments tend to have no union representation or much more flexible contracts.[51]

The idea that unions would look at these results and consider less restrictive contracts, breaking up their union into smaller pieces, or lowering expenses tied to salaries and contract negotiations is mere fantasy. As we've seen in Los Angeles and San Diego, they will fight hard and keep winning, even as children and would-be reformers keep losing.

CONVERSATION WITH CAPRICE YOUNG

During my four-year tour of duty as the United States secretary of education, I traveled extensively throughout the nation. I visited forty-seven of our nation's fifty states—missing only Hawaii, North Dakota, and Vermont—making multiple visits to 75 percent of them. During these visits, I met wonderful people who worked diligently to change the culture of our system of education and to create educational opportunities for kids who were being left behind. But even as I, with deep appreciation, reflect on the wonderful commitment and dedication of these magnificent people whom I had an opportunity to meet, one stands out. Her name is Caprice Young. Young lives in California and, at one time, was president of the school board of the Los Angeles Unified School District. Here are her words:

My mother was one of the early members of United Teachers-Los Angeles in the 1970s. I grew up revering teachers and believing that teachers' unions are vital. Their involvement certainly led to profound improvements in the quality of life for teachers and their families; they rescued teachers from arbitrary management decisions. Collectively, the teachers' unions in California have fought successfully for profound increases in, and protection of, funding for education and, especially, school facilities. However, the system of laws and regulations at the state level, and the hundreds of pages of local labor contract agreements, have completely tied school districts in a Gordian Knot so tight and complex that rational management and governance are virtually impossible.

A quick example from my school board presidency: Once, the teachers and principal of a local high-performing, predominantly Title-I-serving middle school came to me with a problem. For years, they had used a block schedule that reserved time on Thursdays for collaboration and an extra long teachers' meeting. Unfortunately, the new union contract that year decreed that teachers' meetings could only be held on Tuesdays. The school's schedule was nearly impossible to change without disrupting the program that was really working for the students and all concerned. I agreed to raise the issue with the superintendent who, after my question bounced around in the bureaucracy for a month, returned to me with the answer that a "verbal side agreement" (@!#!) precluded them from having meetings on any day but Tuesdays. I returned incredulous to the school with the answer, and we (the school union representative, principal, and I) agreed that we needed to meet with the union president. We took with us a petition signed by nearly all of the teachers from that campus. His secretary directed us to the union vice president who informed us that she could not consider breaking the verbal side agreement ban on meeting day waivers because she had no staff to process such waivers, and if she did it for one school, then seven hundred others would want waivers too. Sigh.

Fast-forward through three months of bureaucratic back-and-forth to two weeks before the start of the semester. I met at a coffee shop with the union president and the local area district superintendent. Together, we all agreed that we would unofficially look the other way if the school were to break the verbal side agreement not to waive the meeting date set by the labor contract. Now, this took this much effort; imagine trying to get something really important done.

Beyond the practical facts of what the teachers' unions have done within government, there is the deeper problem with the political tactics they use to get their way. A small minority (two thousand or so out of more than forty thousand) of extremely active unionists bully and threaten people they believe aren't controlled by them—even potential friends. They are not able to form alliances with people who sometimes disagree with them despite general common cause. . . .

[For example] early in my board term, I worked closely with the political director of the union to implement a phonics-based reading program in the poorly performing elementary schools. His daughter, a teacher, had piloted the curriculum and brought great credibility to an otherwise difficult decision to implement. With support from several union leaders, I increased funding for the arts and after-school programs and started a multibillion dollar school facilities building effort to modernize existing schools and build seats for more than 150,000 students—all in fiscally responsible ways. We did good, important work together, at first.

However, in 2000, we parted ways over the contract renewal. The late nineties were a huge boom time for California and government revenues raced upward. This was a cycle with which I was all too familiar, as a former budget director for the county transportation authority. I had lived through the crash of the early nineties that followed closely after the boom of the late eighties. Back then, I learned a simple truth: government revenue cycles lag the general economy by about eighteen months, both up and down. Back in 1989, the school district leaders gave the teachers a 24 percent increase and within three years were back asking them to take a 10 percent cut. In March 2000, I was working in the technology sector when the dot-com bubble burst, and I watched our businesses flee to Texas during the 2000 summer energy crisis.

By September 2000, when we were in union negotiations, I knew the coming years were going to be really bad. The union and state leadership, on the other hand, felt flush because they were busy riding the tax revenues from the economy's boom of the recent years. We could have used the opportunity to set aside the new $270 million to offset the massive workers compensation reserve or health-care retiree benefits' shortfalls—one-time support for employees that would help the budget in the short and longer terms. Instead, the union was asking for a 20 percent-plus raise in addition to the usual step increases. I objected, recommending a raise at a level more sustainable. The superintendent, who had been on the job three months and was very concerned about getting crosswise with the union, brought us a contract with a 15 percent increase all in one year. Three out of seven of us on the board continued to raise concerns.

At a hearing held at a Westside middle school, the union packed the hall with more than one thousand activists wearing red shirts. They chanted throughout the board meeting and shouted down anyone who spoke. Afterward, several of them surrounded me on my way back to my car. At first, it seemed like a good opportunity for me to make peace and have a dialog with some of the activists. But they quickly began yelling at me and asking me why my children didn't go to public schools. They wouldn't let me respond that one was an infant and the other in preschool and so were too young. Instead, they started physically poking me and saying that they knew where my kids went to school and that I should watch out. My aide yanked me away to my car. Over the following few days, my daughter's preschool received threatening phone calls from people asking about her and telling the receptionist to watch out.

I'm neither the first nor the last to experience this kind of treatment from the people who are supposed to be role models for our children. In 2002, during the biennial redistricting hearings, the unions came early to pack the seats and again shouted down anyone, even students, who disagreed with their views. They booed people they didn't even know, based solely on bizarre prejudices. When truths they don't appreciate are published, they attack. Once a reporter asked how much teachers get paid. I gave him the salary schedule and pointed out that many teachers take on multiple assignments (like substitute teaching during summer vacation), allowing 10 percent of them to earn more than $80,000 per year. The hate mail from unionists was voluminous because they interpreted this as a statement that I felt teachers were overpaid.

Politicians have learned not to cross unions, ever, or they will face personal attack and highly funded opposition during campaigns wherein the union uses outright lies for its purposes. I strongly believe in standing up for what is right, ensuring free speech and political activism. The unions' actions are not tactics in the tradition of social justice and public speech; they are aggressive, violent, and immoral. And each teacher in Los Angeles pays about $680 per year to ensure this continues, whether they want to or not, since agency fees are mandatory even for teachers who don't join.

I went into public service with very idealistic goals. I work with charter schools now so I can support and promote the rights of educators who focus on ensuring student achievement as an act of social justice. I still believe that our public schools can be havens for innovation and caring in pursuit of student excellence. Schools should be centers of the community, where each stakeholder is heard and roles are respected. Most teachers I know want smart, visionary principals who include them in direction setting, but make tough decisions. Parents want to be welcomed onto campus and engaged appropriately in support of their children. Students want to be challenged by creative teachers with high expectations and top teaching skills. Education at its best is a partnership, not a battle.

A Slice of a Parent's Life on the School Board— A Conversation with Jan LaChapelle

While problems with the Los Angeles Unified School District (or to a lesser extent the San Diego School District) might seem like the natural by-product of excessively large school districts or corrupt city officials, the truth is that they are not far removed from the core problems surrounding typical negotiations of teachers' contracts. According to the Society for the Advancement of Excellence in Education, "The outcomes of industrial bargaining in our schools are well known:

- Rigid class size, work schedules, and personnel classifications that prohibit creative ways to meet specific learning needs
- The eroding ability of administrators to manage their schools
- Seniority clauses that prevent the flexibility to have the right teacher in the right place
- Schools with little ability to design appropriate site-based professional development to assist them in achieving their goals for students
- A salary grid lacking incentives for teacher excellence, preventing schools from rewarding skilled professionals for extra effort and success
- Teacher evaluation that has not kept pace with rigorous personnel evaluation practices in other sectors."[52]

So when negotiating contracts, how does the average school board member prevent these problems from becoming further entrenched? If you ask anyone who's ever been on a school board, this prevention is next to impossible.

Jan LaChapelle was on the school board in Bend, Oregon, for eleven years. The Bend-LaPine School District in many ways couldn't be further removed from the situation in Los Angeles. The school district occupies most of rural Deschutes County—an area larger than Delaware, with just over one hundred thousand people in it. The student population is relatively well-off economically and the racial make-up is very homogenous. It would be a stretch to say that LaChapelle is representative of your average volunteer school board member. If anything, the conditions of her school district are quite favorable compared to others.

Despite these advantages over messy urban school districts, negotiating teachers' contracts is as combative there as it is in larger urban school districts where there are far more students and much more money at stake. The core problems surrounding negotiating teachers' contracts are fundamental and systemic. It would be an understatement to say that unions view collective bargaining as little more than a means to promote their own selfish special interests.

The only guardians against total abuse of the system are volunteer, part-time school board members, such as LaChapelle, who have to do battle against an army of full-time union organizers and lawyers earning six-figure salaries. "By and large school board members are volunteers and they're there because they believe in education," says LaChapelle. "So you have two groups that are across the bargaining table from each other for reasons that are diametrically opposed."[53]

For LaChapelle, a mother of three students during her tenure on the school board, this was not encouraging. "I was very quickly disabused of my naiveté. It was a real slap in the face, a real awakening. I started realizing at that time that people who have bought into union mentality really don't really care about kids. I have no quarrel with the teachers' union as a business—that's precisely what it is. But most of us don't think of it in those terms unless we're up against it. As a business, teachers' unions are very, very good at what they do, but to purport to be there for any other reason is a lie.

"During my 11-year tenure on the local school board, we were in negotiations with the union almost continuously. I remember the first of the negotiations; I was designated as a representative of the school board to be on the negotiating team. I remember vividly sitting across the table from people I had seen in my children's classrooms and hearing from them that they didn't care how big the class sizes got, that we needed to give them more money to increase their salaries and that they would deal with cutbacks later."

Pacific Research Institute conducted a study of teachers' union contracts in California and concluded the same thing—that indeed the teachers' union contract frequently demands a "clash with student achievement. Indeed, a direct correlation can be made between teachers and the students' ability to learn if a collective bargaining provision reduces direct teaching time, instructional planning time, or time for student evaluation."[54]

That is frequently what negotiating teachers' contracts comes down to. "School districts have a box of dollars with a limited amount of money in it," says LaChapelle. "But you have a box of dollars and the teacher's union comes in and says it wants their teachers' salaries to go up by a certain percentage every year. Well, if your box of dollars doesn't get bigger every year, that's a real problem. And they don't care if you have to cut the number of teachers there are to grow bigger the salaries of the teachers that are left. What that means are things like cutting teachers, support services, and increasing class sizes. How in the world is that good for kids?"

But that's just the beginning of the headaches she faced as a school board member. Once the unions made it clear that they would only accept increasing teacher salaries at any cost, they then blamed the school board for any negative outcomes regarding students. After unions make salary increases nonnegotiable, consequences be damned, they duck and cover. "The very same people who are on the negotiating team will then go out to the public and say that this school board is going to increase class sizes," says LaChapelle. "How disingenuous is that?"

And that's when dealings between the school board and the unions are working to the unions' favor. During tense contract negotiations, LaChapelle's kids were harassed in school by *teachers*. While the teachers' unions can't be held responsible for the actions of a few rogue teachers, the bare-knuckled, take-no-prisoners attitude toward contract negotiations certainly encourages this kind of shameful behavior among certain union members. However, LaChapelle took this behavior in stride. "Teachers who are highly involved with students and their daily activities are not as likely to participate in these teams because they lack the time to be involved in union stuff."

What was a little more disconcerting was the day that the Deschutes County sheriff showed up on LaChapelle's doorstep with a summons. After the Bend-LaPine School Board began allowing charter schools, the union sued the school board—not just as a public entity, but as individuals, targeting their personal assets. "These are not the kind of tactics that belong with education," says LaChapelle. "A few more incidents like this and no one is going to want to serve on a school board."

Unfortunately, teacher contract negotiations only seem to be getting more tense and difficult in many places. After decades of making concessions to teachers, there's nothing left to cut, no more money to be found. So, contracts only become more difficult to resolve.

On 15 January 2004, the state of Minnesota had more than three-quarters of its teachers' contracts unsettled—Minnesota even has a law on the books that cuts state aid to a district by $25 a pupil if contracts are not settled by that date. The legislature has mercifully suspended that penalty the last two times around, in 2002 and 2004, because the problems of settling contracts are so widespread.[55] Even so, that's a lot of pressure to capitulate for local school boards. Such pressure also serves as an excuse for unions to drag out negotiations knowing full well that school boards are between a rock and a hard place if they don't meet union demands. Minnesota is just one of several states that has had statewide problems settling teacher contracts.

Thankfully, things seem to have changed for the better in the Bend-LaPine school district over the past few years, and LaChapelle finds that incoming school board members seem to be having a less difficult time negotiating teachers' union contracts to the mutual benefit of teachers and students alike. Perhaps this is a sign of hope for other districts. Unfortunately, however, I remain skeptical that the contractual tensions between school boards and unions will be fully resolved any time soon.

UNION IMPEDIMENTS TO REFORM

During my interactions with school districts and superintendents, I have observed many situations where union-imposed work rules were so onerous to my colleagues as to not only impede efforts at effective reform but also to drain scarce district resources, which were needed urgently in the classroom.

In the year 2000, the Buffalo Public School (BPS) system, in New York, was one of the most unionized public school systems in the United States. It had nine unions![56] There was virtually no part of the system's operations that was not covered by union regulations: different unions represented principals and administrators, food services employees, blue-collar employees, clerical and professional staff, building engineers, teachers' aides, bus aides, and substitute teachers. In fact, of the 7,021 employees of this 48,000 student school system, only the superintendent and six other employees were *not* members of one of the nine unions.[57]

The BPS school officials supervising the personnel department—the unit charged with hiring and firing BPS employees—were all union members. This arrangement gave the unions nearly total control over BPS personnel—rendering district accountability efforts impotent and nearly meaningless. An outside observer described the situation perfectly:

> It was ludicrous. The superintendent couldn't hire or fire anyone. The personnel director was a union member, for heaven's sake. How was the superintendent supposed to clean house or demand change when the members of her own management team were in a union with the people they were supposed to be disciplining?[58]

Yet the clearest example of the union's choke hold on the Buffalo Public Schools could be found in the Buffalo Teachers Federation's (BTF) contract during this period. The contract contained language that prohibited the district from inquiring about a teacher's retirement plans—thereby denying the district information about when a teacher intended to retire. This union contract language made it very difficult, if not impossible, for the district to effectively plan to fill teacher vacancies, or even to recruit new faculty. This type of union-imposed management poses a heavy burden on any attempt at improving school district operational efficiency. And when our students are failing and schools are failing to reform—this is a mortal burden.

Of course, the union choke hold over the BPS system happened gradually. Through the years, union influence over district operations grew as the unions won concession after concession from the school board during contract negotiations. It seemed that during this period, each time the board found itself strapped for dollars, in lieu of meeting higher union salary demands, board officials tended to accede to union demands for more influence over district operations. It didn't take long before the board had negotiated itself out of a position of any meaningful influence. While searching for an effective negotiating strategy for the 2000 union negotiations, Patricia Pancoe, BPS's labor negotiator, put the situation in perspective when she observed:

> I don't know exactly what happened in the 1970s or 1980s . . . but I guess the district felt that it was short on money so it decided to give the union everything it could that didn't have a monetary cost. The result is a union contract that's into everything. And now we've got a budget crisis and no money to buy anything back.[59]

A crisis indeed. You can bet that the Buffalo Public School system is not the only school system experiencing this kind of crisis.

The Buffalo Public School system faced teachers' unions who, like most other teachers' unions, buried their iron-fist tactics in the velvet glove of their self-proclaimed advocacy for children. And like so many other teachers' unions, they were always careful to wrap themselves in the time-honored and beloved term *teacher*. But reality did not match their rhetoric.

At 7:00 a.m., on Thursday, 7 September 2000, Philip Rumore, the leader of Buffalo's largest union, the Buffalo Teachers Federation, stood on the steps of BTF's headquarters and announced that the BTF was on strike, effective immediately.[60]

Granted, this strike was called after some really difficult contract discussions. But calling a strike at seven o'clock in the morning is clearly *not* something an organization that is concerned about children would do. At 7:00 a.m. on this school day, many children rode on buses headed for school, oblivious to what awaited them. Some children were already at the school. At 7:00 a.m., many parents had already gone to work, thinking that their children were in the watchful care of their teachers.

This is hardly the mark of a responsible organization whose first concern is the welfare of children. For anyone who doubts the real mission of teachers' unions, look no further than the hardball tactics. Clearly, their first concern is NOT children but the power of the organization.

If you think that this action and its timing was simply a union slip-up, and not a deliberate union negotiation tactic, you need to know that after major pressure from Buffalo's mayor, many parents, and other public officials, the teachers came back to work the next day. And to send the message of disruption and power yet again, one week later on 14 September at exactly 7:05 a.m., the union called another strike.[61]

$\boxed{6}$

UNION CORRUPTION—
BETRAYING TEACHERS

From the very beginning, 2003 looked like it would shape up to be a bad year for teachers' unions. Just a month before the New Year began, a scandal was to erupt that would embroil teachers' union officials and signal the contempt many in union leadership felt toward their teacher members and the public at large. December 2002 began with federal law enforcement implicating the leadership of the Washington DC Teachers Union (WTU), a local affiliate of the powerful American Federation of Teachers. WTU president Barbara Bullock, her assistant, a former WTU treasurer, and a handful of relatives and cronies were caught in a conspiracy to commit money laundering, after embezzling $5 million in compulsory dues wrung from local teachers.[1]

But this case—and its many turns and complicated subplots—was just the beginning. In the Chinese calendar, 2003 was the Year of the Goat. For many teachers, 2003 was the year of the sacrificial lamb, and it was their political leadership that was sharpening their knives. All over the country, teachers' union scandals showed why their partisan leadership opposed accountability for schools; why they resisted any accountability to the public, the government, or their own members; and just what was at stake if those inquiries were allowed to go forward.

By the spring of 2003, the details of the Washington DC scandal began to take form. They painted a sinister picture of graft, lust for power, and deceptive conduct: the AFT's local affiliate president Bullock and a handful of her conspirators used the lack of transparency in their union finances to live lives of the rich and contemptuous.

Bullock's misdeeds began as early as November 1995, when she began to embezzle. It is a measure of the political protection and lack of media oversight that Bullock continued on this path unabated for the next seven years. Bullock never seemed to leave home without her WTU American Express. There were shopping sprees at high-end stores like Neiman Marcus, Saks Fifth Avenue, and the ultraposh Bergdorf Goodman. She loaded her home with items paid for by DC's teachers (and indirectly, the taxpayers), including a $57,000 Tiffany tea service set for twenty-four, a $20,000 custom-tailored mink coat, a $13,000 plasma television set, and a $5,500 Baccarat crystal vase.[2] One of the coconspirators indicted in the case for laundering checks from the Washington Teachers' Union scandal was Bullock's chauffeur, who was paid a salary collected from teachers that soared above $105,000. It's no wonder this chauffeur aided and abetted Bullock; he was paid more than any other union official, save Bullock herself.[3]

All this would have been just another example of union graft were it not for the added tragedy that Bullock ostensibly represented the teachers in one of the most dysfunctional districts in the nation: Washington DC. As Barbara Bullock jetted around town in a $20,000 mink coat, and enjoyed pampering by her $105,000 chauffeur, many of the district's schools were short on books, despite the fact that the district was already spending $8,500 per student as early as 1996.[4] While all this was going on, union members were being lied to,[5] the landlord of their downtown headquarters had to sue to get unpaid rent,[6] and payments to insurance programs for union retirees were not being met.[7]

Bullock was ultimately sentenced to nine years in prison and ordered to pay $4.6 million in restitution to the WTU. But for teachers and parents reading this book, the outrage isn't just Bullock's arrogance. It is the fact that teachers' union officials have built a system and a union movement so contemptuous of the high ideals of education that they are entrusted to protect. They have been able to act with little accountability while millions of children are falling behind; meanwhile the administration and the bureaucracy expand at the expense of teachers. And unfortunately the teachers are the ones who suffer the dire consequences of a system that routinely uses unproven curricula, fails to enforce basic discipline, and does little more than advocate more spending. Such scandals prove that our public education system is a system of perverse incentives that place selfishness and political power before the needs of students and parents.

Of course, it would be unfair to claim that one egregious example characterizes the entire teachers' union movement. But 2003 alone had plenty more indicators of the health of teachers' unions. Just five months after the AFT's Washington scandal, the Miami-Dade School District was mired in its own tale of corruption and contempt. In May of 2003, Pat Tornillo, head of the Miami-Dade affiliate of the AFT—the United Teachers of Dade (UTD)—became the subject of an FBI investigation. The details that emerged were in many respects shockingly similar to the WTU incident. Pat Tornillo was also financing an opulent lifestyle on the compulsory dues siphoned from teachers' salaries.[8]

An audit found that beginning in 1996, Tornillo and other union leaders stole or diverted $3.5 million in union funds.[9] (Note, once again, how far back the scandal went and how long it took to hold the official accountable—seven years.) Though Tornillo too was eventually convicted, few teachers would ever get recompensed for the $2.5 million that he siphoned. His spending spree included: $650,000 for cruises; luxury vacations to the Sydney Olympics, the Far East, and the Caribbean;[10] a personal housekeeper; household bills;[11] jewelry; antiques; artwork; liquor; clothing[12] . . . the list goes on.

Like Bullock's, Tornillo's expensive purchases indicate a depth of corruption close to Enron's corporate raiders. As one newspaper scathingly catalogued these indulgences, "Python-print PJs from Neiman's that cost $173.73? Done. Jewels and other baubles worth $14,334 for wife Donna purchased on exclusive St. Bart's? No prob. A three-week jaunt to Indonesia on pricey Seaborne Cruise Line for $71,000? Sign right here and send the bill to the UTD. What, it's too much trouble to go to your Brickell Key condo during teacher contract negotiations? Then check into the Mandarin Oriental a few yards away and charge it to the union. Cost: $20,056.18."[13]

And just like the WTU scandal, the UTD scandal in Florida belied further economic problems lurking under the surface. The union had an operating budget in excess of $10 million and had recently built a $20 million headquarters in downtown Miami under Tornillo's watch.[14] But the day the scandal broke, several banks immediately tried to reclaim $2.5 million in loans, putting the union in an awkward financial position.[15]

Scandals like these might appear to be isolated examples of individual greed. But they are symptoms of deeper problems in our education system and reveal just how powerful and disconnected teachers' unions are. In fact, unions oppose nearly every meaningful reform, and they can fight long after elections are won by reformers because their pockets are so deep. Although the law requires the union to inform its members if their dues are being spent on political activities (and permits members to withhold dues being used for such purposes), there is little transparency in how compulsory dues are spent.[16]

In short, the same lack of accountability and contempt for openness that allow teachers' union officials to wage partisan wars and pile up personal gifts for years and years also allows them to suppress independent-minded teachers, fight basic, good-government accountability, and duck their responsibilities to the teachers they claim to represent.

Union Leadership: Getting Rich on the Backs of Teachers

While those involved in the teachers' unions would like to have you believe that these two cases of union corruption are aberrations, the unfortunate reality is that they are not. A good case can certainly be made about how unions have advanced the cause of the American worker. Unfortunately, much of the goodwill earned by unions has been tarnished by their reputation for corruption. While the NEA or AFT hasn't cavorted with the mob, almost all unions have some level of endemic corruption; teachers' unions are no exception.

However, teachers' unions have always been well served by the contrast between themselves and more traditional unions. Many Americans still think fondly of unions in theory, if not in practice. The contrast between the negative public perception of, say, the Teamsters and the less ostensibly violent teachers' unions has always benefited teachers' unions. The public's image of teachers is usually that of the underpaid and long-suffering person with a brilliant and creative mind who inspired us to take chances and embrace careers that now define who we are.

So teachers themselves are the teachers' unions' most valuable publicity asset. Interaction with a local teacher, or a union member, is likely all the contact that most people will have with a teachers' union. In every union context, a huge difference exists between the integrity of union *members* and the integrity of union *leadership*. Nowhere is that distinction more clear than in teachers' unions.

After the Tornillo scandal broke, the *Miami Herald* sent a reporter to the home of a Miami teacher named Juan Carlos Martinez. Martinez is an immigrant from the Dominican Republic. He has a master's degree in education and had been teaching for ten years. He has three kids, a mortgage, and a mini-van. He earned $38,050 a year as a teacher and worked a second job as a security guard. He paid $843 a year in union dues (believed to be the highest in the nation[17]), though he couldn't really afford it. When the Tornillo scandal broke, Martinez and other UTD teachers hadn't seen a raise in two years; meanwhile, insurance premiums had gone through the roof. Martinez paid a whopping $639 a month in health insurance—about a fifth of his pay.[18] So, what exactly was Martinez getting from his union in the first place?

It was no wonder then that when the Tornillo scandal broke, the article was headlined, "A Teacher Feels the Sting of Betrayal." "Tornillo was living the life he wanted to and not taking care of [his] business, which was taking care of us," said Martinez. "It felt like a slap in the face." Martinez didn't give up teaching, but the scandal certainly shook his faith. "When I started, I had this naive idea that I could make a difference," said Martinez. "Now? Now, I'm not so sure."[19]

As time passes and unions become even more firmly entrenched in education, the gulf between people like Tornillo and Martinez is bound to increase. As long as unions oppose the ability of schools to reward dedicated teachers with performance pay, unions will seem to be the only hope for higher pay.

Yet such unions rob their teachers blind. The same year Martinez brought home a hard-won and inadequate salary under $40,000 for teaching, Tornillo had a base salary of $228,000 and a $43,000 expense account in 2003.[20] Such salary imbalance, understandably, is not widely advertised, and information about local union spending is incredibly hard to access. Thus, few teachers knew that Tornillo had an expense account higher than most of their salaries. Despite a combined bankroll of $271,000 a year, Tornillo still felt entitled to another $2.5 million from his members.[21]

While I firmly believe that individuals are accountable for their own crimes, I can't help but wonder how much the union environment inculcated this behavior. One cannot look at Bullock's and Tornillo's respective crimes and see them as necessarily independent of each other, or of their union. Aside from the startlingly similar nature of their crimes, both Bullock and Tornillo weren't local rogues; both had worked for the AFT on the national level. Both got away with their crimes for so long, not because they were clever or ingenious, but because over very long periods of time there was no managerial oversight or financial accountability within the organization.

Even when their brazen crimes were impossible for others to ignore, they continued to get away with them because others feared the union's absolute power.[22] Again a culture of fear was palpable in both cases. According to the *Washington Post,* in the case of Barbara Bullock:

> Some union employees who suspected improprieties stayed quiet for fear of losing their jobs, according to a source with knowledge of the probe. "It's all part of the culture at the union office, but it goes deeper than Barbara Bullock," said George Parker, a teacher and union activist who unsuccessfully ran against her twice. He plans to seek the presidency again this year. "It's a culture that is just unbelievable—of financial secrecy, of manipulation of information," Parker said. "The problem is that everybody just let it happen."[23]

The culture and environment surrounding Tornillo didn't sound any less autocratic. Tornillo was very powerful, and was frequently referred to as a kingmaker without whose support it was nearly impossible to get anything done. According to one observer, in the *Orlando Sentinel*:

> "[Tornillo is] a despot. He believes he owns the organization the same way Castro believes he owns Cuba," said [Damaris] Daugherty, executive director of the Teacher Rights Advocacy Coalition. "

We've been screaming it for years: The union is taking our money to fund their lavish lifestyles. Everybody is getting rich on the backs of teachers."[24]

Even when the crimes are obvious to those around the union, the general feeling is that nothing can be done about it—at least not without the very real fear of retribution. So what prevents this kind of abuse of power from happening again? What safeguards are in place so that the teachers like Juan Carlos Martinez won't be robbed and taken for granted by union leaders in the future? Unfortunately, there is next to nothing in the way of legal safeguards.

Union officials are enabled by law to require all teachers in a bargaining unit to pay union dues.[25] If a teacher vehemently disagrees with union policy or, say, massive corruption by union leadership, they simply have no choice but to pay union dues or quit. If you're in favor of a specific political issue and the teachers' union supports the opposing view with your dues, too bad. If you're a Republican and don't like the teachers' unions near-exclusive support of Democrats, too bad.

It also makes the unions supremely arrogant. No matter how mismanaged they are, they don't have to worry about funds drying up. Just how arrogant are they? Even when they are caught red-handed robbing union members, union leadership feels little or no compulsion to make up for their mismanagement.

After vowing in the *Washington Post* that the WTU would "work to recoup the money and return it to the teachers," "National" Saunders, a teacher from Anacostia Senior High School in DC, sued the AFT and WTU to reclaim the funds that were robbed from DC teachers by Bullock and her cronies.[26]

Here's how the judge in the case summed up how monies would be repaid: The national AFT would "provide an aggregate 'loan' of $250,000" (of $5 million in missing funds) to the 1,700 teachers who requested reimbursement. But the local WTU would have to repay the loan—plus interest. Makes sense, right? However, the money being repaid to the national affiliate was going to come straight out of the teachers' compulsory union dues![27]

Or as the judge in the case dryly noted, "That's not a repayment, is it?"[28]

In this case, the teachers' only recourse would be to resign their formal membership from the union, at which point they could demand an audit and ask for a refund of all union dues not directly related to collective bargaining.

This last incident perfectly encapsulates how decades of political corruption in teachers' unions have ensured that such unions are legally protected and not to be held accountable for their gross mismanagement and abuse of power. Though personal corruption may be an ongoing problem within union ranks, I view this as an outgrowth of teachers' unions' reprehensible lobbying practices. And this method of operating doesn't just negatively impact America's teachers; it harms every American and goes to the very core of our political process.

THE NEA AND CORRUPTION, OR POLITICS AS USUAL

The two examples discussed above involved independent employees and their failure of personal ethics. But it is important to view these incidents in a larger context. To the extent that the AFT has created a union culture in which a lack of accountability and disrespect for the membership can easily lead to corruption, I believe this is a grievous situation that needs to be addressed. In the NEA, the problem seems not to be so much about individual employees abusing their responsibilities. Rather, dodging accountability and operating underhandedly appear to be *standard operating procedure*. What do I mean by this? It seems quite clear that the NEA's leadership has been pursuing, virtually unchallenged, a carefully orchestrated strategy of using money that is supposed to be used to advance teachers' interests through collective bargaining to instead pursue the union's partisan political interests. As discussed earlier, not only does the NEA divert funds paid by its members, often without their awareness and approval, it also robs millions from taxpayers every year by failing to pay taxes on its political activities.

Inside its palatial Washington headquarters is a framed quote from Florida Democrat, Senator Bob Graham: "No presidential candidate who wants to win in November ignores the National Education Association anymore."[29] Indeed, Mark Levin's enterprising work and the NEA's own comments reveal the National Education Association to be one of the most powerful and deceptive political organizations working in DC.

Yet, despite this undeniable record of intense political activity, the NEA still enjoys exemption from taxation through its status as a non-profit organization. Although the Internal Revenue Service requires nonprofits to report and pay taxes on all political expenditures (at the higher corporate rate, incidentally), the NEA has skirted these require-ments.[30] By way of comparison, other politically active nonprofits, such as the National Association of Manufacturers and the United States Chamber of Commerce, spent millions on political activities, declared them, and paid taxes on them.

So what did Levin and Landmark unearth? The NEA during this period of time spent:

- $400,000 for voter registration records and political databases in 1994
- $2.2 million in 1996–97 to "increase the association's capacity to provide assistance to recommended candidates"
- $872,535 for "state-specific campaign . . . aimed at electing bipartisan pro-education candidates" in the 1998 election

- $400,000 to the Washington state NEA affiliate to help defeat school voucher and charter school initiatives
- $4.9 million for the 2000 election for such things as "organizational partnerships with political parties, campaign committees and political organizations"

And the list goes on and on.[31]

The IRS clearly defines political expenditure as one "in connection with: influencing legislation; participating or intervening in any political campaign on behalf of (or in opposition to) any candidate for public office; attempting to influence the general public with respect to elections, legislative matters, or referendums; and any direct communication with a covered executive branch official in an attempt to influence the person's official actions or positions."[32] There's little room for ambiguity in that statement, especially given what the NEA has done and continues to do. And despite the egregious violations that we do know about, the problem could potentially be much bigger than we realize.

Little is known about the full extent of the NEA's political activities, and Levin has rightly argued that the NEA's 1,800 UniServ workers are really political operatives involved in "developing and/or executing local association political action." UniServ comprises "the largest army of campaign workers that any organization has"—more than the staffs of the Republican National Committee and the Democratic National Committee put together.[33] Hard numbers are difficult to come by, but consider that former NEA and AFT member Myron Lieberman estimates that the NEA has annual revenues of over a billion dollars.[34] Given the number of employees that are essentially political operatives and their related expenses, in addition to millions of dollars in direct contributions to national candidates, money spent on local and state campaigns, and the general zeal that the NEA has for the Democratic Party, it might be a very conservative estimate to suggest that a tenth of the NEA's annual budget is spent on political activities as defined by the IRS.

That would amount to over $100,000,000 annually—100 million tax-free dollars. This situation places the NEA in a highly hypocritical position, as it repeatedly claims that education programs are under-funded, and as its Democratic allies frequently argue that loopholes allow too many corporations to avoid paying sufficient taxes.

THE NEA AND DEMOCRATS: TO SERVE AND PROTECT

How has the NEA gotten away with such egregious violations for so long? The reason the group has not been fully exposed and prosecuted for being a political operation is precisely because it is a political organization. The NEA doesn't donate to and *help* the Democratic Party; the NEA (and the AFT) donates to and *dominates* the Democratic Party.

Thanks to Landmark, we know just how political the very organization of the NEA is. The four-year investigation of the AFL-CIO, conducted by the Federal Election Commission (FEC), subpoenaed thousands of internal documents relating to the coordination of unions and the Democratic Party. Knowing that the NEA was mentioned several times in these documents, Landmark Legal Foundation requested copies of all of the information subpoenaed in the investigation. It was a public investigation, and making all of the information public would have been normal procedure. Despite the fact that the judge had ruled that there was no evidence of anything incriminating, the FEC, still under purview of the Democratic Clinton administration, dragged their feet in releasing the documents involved in the investigation. They claimed that there was a microfiche problem, that there were too many documents, and so forth. Finally, after Landmark Legal Foundation threatened to sue, six thousand documents were released. Landmark Legal Foundation swept in and made copies just in time. Due to political pressure, the documents were ordered resealed just four days later.[35]

Fortunately, by then Landmark had gotten what they needed—hard evidence and a rare glimpse inside the most powerful political group in the nation. The NEA claims, of course, to be a bipartisan, proeducation group that should be exempt from federal taxes. It tries to portray itself as a rather innocuous advocacy group protecting America's beleaguered teachers, with nary a reference to hardball politics. As the NEA Web site states:

> From its headquarters in Washington, DC, NEA lobbies Congress and federal agencies on behalf of its members and public schools, supports and coordinates innovative projects, works with other education organizations and friends of public education, provides training and assistance to its affiliates. . . .[36]

Landmark's official complaint summarizing the thousands of pages of internal NEA documents tells a different story: it is the story of a partisan juggernaut wringing dues from members to pursue political efforts that limit parental choices, undermine student options, and destroy meaningful standards and accountability in education.[37]

For example, Landmark's court documents state, "Review of NEA publications reveal the overwhelming importance it attributes to political activity as a core purpose of the union's existence."[38] In the introduction of "How to Set Up and Operate a Local Association Political Action Program," the NEA clearly states its purpose:

> In too many places, from too many quarters, public schools and teachers are under attack. We face great issues: tuition tax credits, education reform, voucher systems, competency testing, academic freedom, collective bargaining, funding cuts and more. *Fighting back means fighting back through politics—practical politics.*[39] (Emphasis added.)

Did you notice that? They included "education reform" as something to fight against! In a section entitled, "Organizing for Political Action," the NEA political action manual states:

> The most effective way in which the Association can achieve significant gains for members and for public education is through *political organizing*. By *helping to elect* pro-education candidates at the local, state and national levels, we can more easily pass or defeat legislative proposals that impact on public education for all.[40] (Emphasis added.)

For the NEA, the compulsory dues collected from members are not strictly separated into union activity and political activity. It is often, by design, one and the same. For instance, the NEA political action handbook has a section on "Integrating Political Action into the Local Association," which states that it is a primary mission of the organization's structure to commingle these funds:

Integrating the Structure

> The Association is ultimately responsible for all of its programs—including political action. In the minds of officeholders, candidates, and the public, it is the Association they are dealing with—not a separate and isolated political action committee.
>
> Consult your state Association to determine the best method of integration. Some political action committees (PACs) have found it effective to name the Association president (or his/her designee) as the committee chair. Often, to foster integration, the UniServ staff serves as a non-voting committee treasurer.
>
> You may want to consider these additional organizational steps which have proved effective in many situations: naming an odd number of members to the PAC; making sure a majority (or significant

number) of the PAC members are also members of the local Association board of directors . . . naming the Association representative . . . of each school building as the political representative.[41]

In addition, the NEA expressly advises PAC fundraisers to blur the distinctions between political action and membership drives.

Combine PAC fundraising and the Association's membership drive, so you avoid separate drives by asking people to join the Association and give to the PAC at the same time. (Building a unified commitment to political action means giving each Association member the opportunity to contribute his/her fair share to PAC.)[42]

The NEA also states that Association publications should "include political action program articles."[43] Not only should NEA structures and programs be fully integrated with political action, but campaigning and politicking never stop: "Political action and lobbying are year-round activities."[44] As Landmark concluded in its court complaint, "The NEA's political guidebooks provide evidence of a systematic strategy to integrate political action in all aspects of union organizations, rather than segregate those activities from general operations."[45]

Does the NEA succeed in this round-the-clock political organizing? If the handbooks state the mission, the NEA budgets show their success. Even a cursory sampling from Landmark's invaluable work reveals the hundreds of thousands of dollars that are transferred from teachers' pocketbooks into the coffers of unaccountable union and party hacks. From Landmark's presentation of the NEA's 1998 to 2000 Strategic Plan and Budget:

- $350,000 for "cyberspace advocacy systems developed and maintained on the NEA and state affiliate Web sites that mobilize Association members and the public in support of pro-public education legislation and *candidates at the state and federal level."* (Id. (emphasis added))

- . . . $9.2 million for "[s]ignificantly increased and lasting bipartisan political advocacy and support for public education."
- $386,000 earmarked for 1999–2000 for "organizational partnerships with political parties, *campaign committees,* and *political organizations representing elected officials at the state and national levels* strengthened, increasing legislators'commitment to support public education on a bipartisan basis." (Id. (emphasis added));
- $540,000 over two years for the development of a "national political strategy developed to address issues such as *congressional and legislative reapportionment and redistricting,* campaign finance reform, *candidate recruitment,* independent expenditures, *early voting, and vote-by-mail programs in order to strengthen support for pro-public education candidates . . ."* (Id. (emphasis added));
- $350,000 for "training programs and materials designed, developed, and tested that *strengthen organizational capacity to support the election of pro-public education candidates . . ."* (Id. (emphasis added));
- $872,000 in each 1998 and 2000 intended to develop a "comprehensive coordinated state-specific campaign developed and implemented [and] aimed at *electing bipartisan pro-education candidates"* in each respective election cycle; (Id. (emphasis added)) and
- $530,000 for "political data systems and services maintained and enhanced to effectively assist state affiliate political programs." (Id.)[46]

In the Program Accomplishment Report of 1994–1995, the NEA clearly set aside more than $2.5 million for "Government Relations program assistance to state affiliates." The group then bragged:

[The] NEA provided coordinated program assistance and consultation to state affiliates in the following areas: affiliate capacity building; training; state legislative assistance; ballot and referenda; *candidate recruitment and recommendation*; campaign staff and support; message development political advocacy (sic); federal legislative support and member mobilization; PAC fundraising; and [*delegate selection*]. Assistance provided to local affiliates through state affiliates on school board and local levy programs.[47] (Emphasis added.)

In passage after passage, in document after document, the NEA prides itself on its political organizing and smash-mouth politics. Collective bargaining is the driving reason unions use to collect compulsory dues, but the NEA's UniServ bargaining agents appear to be packed with political partisans. The 1,800 UniServ directors are on the ground working at, among other things:

Developing and/or executing local association political action, community development, community/public relations, legislative support and professional development activities and programs . . . and coordinating and advocating national and state association programs and priorities with local associations and members.[48]

In addition, the NEA's publication, *How to Raise Money for NEA-PAC Education's Defense Fund*, instructed UniServ directors to do the following:

- Manage all political activities within their unit;
- Coordinate UniServ activities with local (NEA-affiliate) PAC chairs;
- Train union PAC representatives and distribute materials; and
- Collect and transmit PAC contributions to the state PAC official within three days.[49]

Not only were these UniServ directors seeking to coordinate with political operations, but they were actively politicizing both sides of union operations. Another Landmark discovery revealed that in the NEA's 1994–1995 Program Accomplishment Report, the NEA disclosed that it expended $310,354 educating and training affiliates in order to "increase their capacity and success in political campaigns."[50] As Landmark wrote the court:

> NEA provided consultation and on-site assistance to build affiliate capacity in conducting successful political campaigns. Staff designed, developed and delivered training; provided strategic assistance on state legislative and ballot issues; and consulted affiliates on campaign strategy and support, polling, message development, and member communication and mobilization. *NEA developed and distributed a three part training series aimed at further developing the capacity of state and local affiliates to elect pro-education candidates, entitled Winning Campaign Strategies; Fundraising Voter Contact, and Volunteers. Sessions were held with UniServ staff to prepare them to deliver the training to local members.*[51] (Emphasis added.)

Remember, all of this work to integrate, coordinate, commingle, and politically co-opt the operations is carried out by an organization supposedly representing teachers in collective bargaining. Such misplaced energy reveals a structure that puts power and politics first, liberal crusades second, teachers' needs third, and children's needs for a good education dead last.

In the conclusion of its invaluable complaint to the court, Landmark summarized the problems and apparent illegalities that the NEA violations create for the IRS, the public, and for the teachers they purport to represent. In sum:

> The evidence indicates that the NEA has failed to report the full extent of its political expenditures on its Form 990 tax returns for 1994, 1995, 1996 and 1997. Moreover, the NEA's failure to account

fully for its political expenditures may be ongoing, implicating future tax return filings.[52]

Landmark has not been the only organization to draw this conclusion. The internal analysis and objective judgment from within the organization is an indictment, too. In 1997, the National Education Association realized that the public was catching on to its truly politically partisan nature. So, the NEA hired the Kamber Group to improve its public relations. After analyzing external perceptions and internal practices, the Kamber Group warned that the NEA was too quick to "dismiss attacks [on the NEA] as the rantings of extremists."[53] The Kamber Group called the report "An Institution at Risk," stating that the NEA "must shift to a crisis mode of operations."[54] Despite the NEA's attacks on any and all critics, concerns about the organization weren't all the result of "anti-labor zealots who jump at every opportunity to bash unions" or "religious extremists who equate public education with Satan."[55]

The Kamber Group said that the image of the NEA was "an inside-the-beltway, highly partisan, 800 pound gorilla."[56] Kamber further stated:

> In many political and legislative battles, the NEA has been well served by this perception [of being a political heavyweight]. . . . But from a message standpoint, it contributes to the notion of the Association as a gargantuan special interest group—and this is not consistent with the objective of portraying the NEA as concerned first and foremost with our children.[57]

It is difficult to see how "a crisis mode of operations" could fix all this. From my perspective as secretary of education, it is not a problem of style; it is a problem of substance. What the Kamber Group study shows, however, is that the NEA is recognized as a political (and politically powerful) special interest group. NEA dismisses critics and reformers as religious cranks and right-wing loons. Sadly, all of my observations in these seven intervening years indicate that nothing has changed.

Landmark's incisive investigation of internal NEA documents revealed an overtly political plan. Kamber's work admitted the politically powerful and successfully partisan NEA tactics. So, what was the Kamber Group's suggestion? Try to make the NEA's political operation look not as partisan:

> We don't want to mess with success, and so we have no significant substantive suggestions about how the NEA makes its members' voices heard in the political and legislative arenas. But we do think politics and government relations should take a lower media profile for a while, with the sole exceptions of occasions when the NEA endorses Republicans.[58]

DRIVING DEMOCRATIC PARTISANSHIP

Obviously, Kamber urged the NEA to cozy up to the Republicans as a way to offset their strong connection to the Democratic Party. Before the Landmark report, NEA appeared to be merely an ardent supporter of the Democratic Party. But both financially and otherwise, the ties were much stronger than that: often ties are actually more like controlling reins on Democratic policy positions. In fact, the portrait of the party that emerged in the documents is that of a wholly owned subsidiary of the NEA. In an interview with radio host Geoff Metcalf, Landmark Legal Foundation's Mark Levin outlined the whole scheme:

> Q: I was blown away when I found out that the NEA wasn't only a participant in a lot of the party-platform things, and so forth, but actually had *veto* power.

A: *That's* the point! This is the structure. They set up a national coordinating committee—steering committee—this is where the wealthiest, most powerful, most influential members sat. They were from the Democratic National Committee in 1996 [which] these documents talk about. They were from the Democratic Senatorial Committee, the Democratic Congressional Committee (meaning the House races), the 1996 Clinton-Gore Committee, the AFL-CIO, Emily's List and, of course, our friends at the NEA. They sat on this national coordinating committee steering committee and *they* decided what the issues would be, how much money would be spent and what the strategy would be.

Q: What is so amazing and appalling was they actually withheld their financial commitment *until* they had input into the policy.

A: [Yes, input] into the policy at the state level. They set up 50 of these same kinds of steering committees in every state where, typically, the state Democratic Party and the affiliates of these national unions—like in Pennsylvania, the Pennsylvania State Education Association and so forth—would sit on these state committees. Candidates would contribute to these committees and these committees would help decide what the strategy would be in congressional races, in gubernatorial races, senatorial races—they would pull the strategy together and *then* they would send it up the ladder to this national committee, we were talking about and this national committee could approve it, modify it, or reject it.[59]

In too many cases, the NEA has veto power over the activities of the Democratic Party. That's how influential they are. While both political parties are beholden to special interests of varying degrees, this is simply beyond the pale. Levin puts this into perspective: "Imagine the outrage if it emerged that the Republican National Committee had given HMOs and the oil companies a veto over the Republican Party platform in exchange for contributions."[60] In fact, that very accusation is frequently leveled—without much credibility—at the Republican Party to score political points. Yet much of mainstream media has been largely silent on the fact that there is concrete proof that the Democrats are the ones most beholden to these pernicious special interest groups. Then again, the media has been woefully negligent in documenting the threat of teachers' unions. So, why would they make this connection?

However, given the existence of such proof, it doesn't seem so far-fetched to suggest that teachers' unions have gotten away with this financial chicanery and influence peddling because they have been actively protected by Democrats. Less than a year after Clinton took office, Debra DeLee, formerly the director of governmental relations at the NEA, became executive director of the Democratic National Committee. Based on the information uncovered in Landmark Legal Foundation's complaints, it's not audacious to suggest that this was the first of many paybacks for helping to elect the first Democratic president in sixteen years.

It's also worth noting that the Clinton administration was frequently accused of employing the IRS for political purposes. The *Washington Times*, the *Wall Street Journal*, and the *Chicago Tribune* all noted that far too many conservative groups and Clinton critics were being audited for it to seem entirely coincidental.[61] This is not a complete list, but during the Clinton administration the Heritage Foundation, National Rifle Association, Western Journalism Center, Citizens Against Government Waste, *National Review*, the *American Spectator*, and the National Center for Public Policy Research were all audited. In the case of the prominent conservative think tank, the Heritage Foundation, though nothing came of their audit, much of the investigation focused on a single incident where Heritage had given the Dole campaign a one-time use of the organization's mailing list.[62] If this did constitute a political expenditure, and it's unclear that it did, it was worth next to nothing compared to what the NEA was spending on Democrats and what they were not paying in taxes that same election cycle. Yet, mysteriously, the NEA escaped the scrutiny of the IRS. (The Clinton administration slashed the budget of the Office of Labor Management Standards, the government entity responsible for union audits. The year George W. Bush took office, government union audits were down from a high of 1,584 in 1984 to just 238.[63])

Still the NEA and the Democratic Party continue to openly flaunt their corrupt relationship. Just one week after Gore conceded defeat in December of 2000, and less than six months after Landmark Legal Foundation filed its complaint documenting corrupt ties between the NEA and the Democratic Party, the Florida Chapter of the National Education Association (FEA) took out an additional $1.7 million mortgage on their headquarters. Again not coincidentally, the FEA spent $1.5 million on Bill McBride's unsuccessful gubernatorial campaign to oust Governor Jeb Bush. It was this financial support that helped the relatively unknown McBride beat out former attorney general Janet Reno in the primaries; it was, however, not enough to win the election. When questioned about this, FEA president Maureen Dinnen said that a May 2001 delegate assembly gave her "not exactly a blank check," but the authority to do whatever could be done to defeat Bush.[64]

Of course, this authority from union members came five months after the $1.7 million mortgage was procured. And the fact that it was taken out one week after Gore conceded defeat in the Florida recount makes it reek of payback on behalf of the Democratic Party, going after the president's brother for the bitter dealings in Florida's presidential election in 2000. Given that McBride lost, on what appears to be a partisan vendetta, and that $1.5 million of union dues were essentially wasted, one has to ask if this kind of stridently political activity is really in the best interests of the Florida Education Association's members.[65]

Thankfully, the Florida Election Commission questioned the NEA's political entanglement in the Bush/McBride election as well. After the Republican members of the commission vindicated themselves, the Florida Election Commission reviewed the FEA's involvement in the McBride campaign in June 2003. They voted 6-3 that there was evidence the FEA and McBride violated state campaign laws. The case was referred to an administrative court and has yet to be resolved as of this writing—McBride and the FEA potentially face millions in fines.[66]

This destructive integration of the NEA and Democratic Party doesn't just exploit teachers but also harms the entire Democratic Party. Because of all the strings attached to the money the NEA gives to the DNC, the NEA stamps out any potential ideological diversity that might make the Democrats more competitive with the Republicans. Bill Bradley was actively attacked by the NEA, as was their candidate Al Gore in the 2000 presidential primary, for supporting school vouchers (vouchers were also supported by Joe Lieberman, a position he had to quietly disown after he signed on to the Gore ticket).[67]

In 2004, while campaigning for president, John Kerry came out in favor of merit pay for teachers, something that the teachers' unions had long opposed. After meeting with the NEA, a few weeks later, Kerry reversed course and promised to never support merit pay for teachers. Given the portrayal of John Kerry, it would be tempting to say that this was one of his patented flip-flops, or that he supported merit pay before he was against it.[68]

But the truth is much more sinister than that. The fact is that it is nearly impossible to run for national office as a Democrat and oppose teachers' union policy. Running for president, while opposing union policy, *is* actually impossible, judging by the last four election cycles. The NEA pumped over one million dollars into the Kerry campaign on mailings alone.[69] Therefore, he had no choice.

I believe that in this case change and reform are inevitable. Increasingly Democrats are finding it more uncomfortable to squelch education reform in exchange for campaign cash. One prominent undecided voter, who wrote on the very popular *Instapundit* blog, attempted to compare Kerry and Bush on the issues. He found that when it came to positions on education, "Bush [won] by a landslide. The Democrats are simply too hostage to the teachers' unions to be even marginally credible on education."[70] This kind of sentiment is becoming increasingly common throughout the country, and I firmly believe it will be a more prominent discussion in future elections.

That is, of course, if the relationship between the teachers' unions and Democrats doesn't implode on its own. Despite the utterly baseless accusations of partisan motivation, the IRS informed the NEA that they would be audited—finally.[71] So who knows what further revelations might be in store? Given what we already know, the results of the audit are unlikely to be encouraging. Still, this is a necessary step for reform.

The IRS announced the audit in September of 2003, and it will likely continue for some time. Did I mention that 2003 was a very bad year for teachers' unions? Many concerned critics almost wish that the corruption in teachers' unions and Democratic Party politics would accelerate so that the pressure for reform would reach critical mass. I'm more positive than that, and I hate to see children harmed in the meantime, waiting around for things to get worse so that they can get better. So, casting a harsh and revealing light on union corruption is necessary for educating the public and undercutting the union's political support.

Here's hoping that the bad years for teachers' unions today means better years for American education tomorrow.

The Electoral Cost of Fighting the Union Monster

I've watched politics long enough to know that far too often elections are about winning and losing, rather than choosing the right law or the right candidate. To the victor goes the spoils, and after the fact, not much thought goes into whether or not the right course of action has been chosen.

I can't think of a better example of how political might can distort an election than in November 2005 when Governor Arnold Schwarzenegger called a special election in California to deal with the state's growing budget crisis and a host of necessary union and education reform issues.

Now, Schwarzenegger has been widely criticized for being out of touch because of this special election, which may have badly damaged his chances for reelection. In fact, a Google search for "Schwarzenegger" and "disastrous special election" turns up 129,000 results.[72] Instead of weighing in on Schwarzenegger's political career—the only barometer that seems to matter to a lot of people—I commend the man for his courage in addressing this volatile issue.

With his state facing a number of crises, he took bold and decisive action in calling a special election, and he made his case directly to the public. Unfortunately, in the ensuing election, he paid dearly for his boldness: every important voter initiative he supported was defeated. Even so, this kind of behavior from politicians should be encouraged. Schwarzenegger would never have had to stick his neck out so far if a generation of California politicians before him had had an ounce of the guts he has. And while the special election is over, the problems the election tried to address have certainly not gone away.

Unfortunately, in the aftermath, all that mattered in the national political calculus was Schwarzenegger's defeat. Not nearly enough hard questions have been asked about how the governor was defeated and whether or not this was a good thing. Pundits often painted a Schwarzenegger whose mistaken ideas and agenda were out of step with the voting public. But these assessments failed to go beneath the surface. Looking closer, I saw a guy who recognized two obvious truths: one, the educational system was broken; and two, unions were corrupting the political process and keeping any budget and educational reform off the table to further stuff their coffers. Unfortunately, Schwarzenegger was victimized by a vulgar display of union power.

Schwarzenegger may have lost the election in ignominious fashion, but he was, and is, right about unions and education. He should sleep a lot better at night than most politicians knowing that he at least tried to bring about change.

At issue in California's special election in November 2005 were four critical measures: Proposition 74, which tried to extend the length of time it took public school teachers to get tenure from two years to five; Proposition 75, which tried to limit union spending on political activities; Proposition 76, which tried to limit state spending; and Proposition 77, which was an attempt to curb gerrymandering in the state.

Proposition 75 was opposed by unions for obvious reasons, and clearly teachers' unions had a vested interest in Proposition 74, about teacher tenure. (According to Patty Armanini, a Marin County teacher, it takes "three to four grueling years" to fire even a clearly incompetent teacher.[73] In other words, California teachers can get tenure in less time than it takes to get them fired. See chapter 4 for more on the difficulty of firing teachers.) Proposition 76 was opposed by unions because a number of unionized public sectors were demanding money they say was "owed" to them, despite the state's budget crisis.

If Schwarzenegger made any major mistake in calling this special election, it was underestimating what lengths to which unions—more specifically, teachers' unions—would go to protect their interests.

In fact, unions spent *$100 million* campaigning against the governor's initiatives.[74] Think about that. In comparison, consider that over the course of about two years, John Kerry and George W. Bush spent over $300 million on their nationwide presidential campaigns.[75] Yet here, the teachers' unions spent $100 million in a *statewide* election, and a special election at that. It is an amazing amount of money, considering the stakes normally involved in a regional election. If proponents of campaign finance reform were really serious, this kind of massive union spending would raise as many red flags as the specter of corporate influence.

Of course, typically hard-nosed union tactics have tried to spin this spending the other way around. "[Schwarzenegger] does owe California an apology for wasting $50 million on a special election that obviously no one wanted, and he owes it to voters for trashing the real working people in California," said Barbara Kerr, head of the California Teachers Association.[76]

It is more than disingenuous to say that no one wanted the election. If no one wanted such reforms, why were unions so concerned that they spent a whopping $100 million campaigning in the election?

Furthermore, when Kerr refers to "the real working people in California," the clear implication is that this issue would somehow affect millions of the state's workers. Yet the reality is that unions in California are a fraction of the populace. Union members make up only 16.8 percent of the state's 14 million workers.[77] Government unions are a fraction of that number. Further subdivide that and you get an even tinier group of teachers' union members. This is remarkable, considering their outsized influence.

"In California, nonunion everyday workers make up 83.2 percent of workers. But they don't pay $50 or $100 in monthly dues into a kitty used to spend $100 million on politics," said the *Daily News of Los Angeles* columnist Jill Stewart. "Voters can only hope that with these 16.8 percenters trying to control the debate, the people elected to represent the broader population will argue vigorously on their behalf."[78]

Ironically, the CTA made a strong case for Schwarzenegger's ballot initiative restricting union political activity in the process of raising that money. In order to raise the cash to fight Arnold, the CTA decided to raise dues an extra $180. This decision, made by top union brass, was done without a vote from the members themselves. Once upon a time, this kind of action would have been unthinkable behavior for a union. Now it's just par for the course.

Nonetheless, it was enough to spark a lawsuit against the CTA. Even with compulsory union dues, members are theoretically allowed to opt out of paying the portion of their dues used in political activity. I say "theoretically" because according to Judy Liegmann, a Bay-area fifth-grade teacher who filed the class action suit against the CTA, "They never asked our permission, nor even informed us of the purpose of the new fee. I found out purely by chance. Furthermore, when I asked for the money to be returned to me, CTA officials indicated that I could have to wait one or two years."[79] In the meantime, the union earns millions through the interest of Liegmann and other teachers' "voluntary donations," while they debate whether to give back money that's not rightfully theirs.

Meanwhile, what happened to the four propositions on the ballot in November 2005? Thanks in no small part to the CTA's expensive opposition campaign, all of them failed on Election Day.[80]

Schwarzenegger has a keen sense of the problems his state faces. And even though he lost the election, he will undoubtedly learn from his political mistakes. In that special election union, opponents, and especially the CTA, conducted themselves in a way that only proved him right. Unfortunately, in California, political might makes right. Hopefully Schwarzenegger and his successors will continue to fight to get tyrannical unions under control because, clearly, something must be done. I worry, however, that Schwarzenegger's experience will scare away other leaders who might otherwise wish to confront the issue.

As it is, far too many politicians are afraid to stand up and do something about the fact that unions have too much influence in elections. As columnist Jill Stewart said, "Unions should have their say. But they are using up all available oxygen."[81]

NEA CONVENTION ACTIVITY FOR 6 JULY 2005

The NEA makes every effort to convince the public that its purpose is to provide for the welfare of teachers. Let's put that claim to the test by examining some of the resolutions that were under consideration on 6 July during the NEA's 2005 convention. Do the issues the delegates worked on that day address the welfare of either children or teachers? Will I give away the answer by pointing out that the interests on this list rival the agendas of the most unrepentantly ideological groups? Decide for yourself.

Here's some of what the delegates did on 6 July 2005:

- Approved new NEA resolutions, with no extraordinary changes to the current ones
- Approved, without debate, an amendment to NEA's policy statement on charter schools that reads, "School districts under state receivership should be ineligible for a charter."
- Approved [New Business Initiative, or NBI] 61, which called on President Bush and Congress to create an exit strategy to end the US military occupation of Iraq
- Approved NBI 63, which commits NEA to educating members about the Central American Free Trade Agreement (CAFTA) "and its serious negative consequences for education"
- Referred NBI 75 to committee, designed to set aside a fragrance-free zone at the [Representative Assembly, or RA]
- Referred NBI 78 to the Executive Committee, to urge members to boycott Wal-Mart
- Approved NBI 81, directing NEA to research the possibility of offering a labor union history training program that emphasizes curriculum for students
- Approved NBI 91, the "alternative to latex" measure after minutes of entertaining debate about the "many satisfactory alternatives to decorative and recreational items containing latex" mentioned in the rationale for the NBI[82]

7

THE THREAT OF
CHARTER SCHOOL SUCCESS

In the summer of 2004, the public and the media were focused on the presidential campaign and the major party conventions. But buried under the national headlines, important developments were in the works over a key educational reform: charter schools. For a brief moment, the public caught a glimpse of just how far the defenders of mediocrity have gone to protect the political status quo.

The public relations (PR) unit at the American Federation of Teachers had long claimed they were an enthusiastic supporter of the idea of charter schools. The PR team pointed to past remarks made by the AFT's visionary president, the late Al Shanker. Shanker, after returning from a trip to Germany, was deeply impressed with an innovative school he had seen on his trip. The idea behind the charter school is to free the school of bureaucracy in exchange for the contractual promise to be held responsible for academic achievement and results. Upon his return to America, Shanker had even spoken out in favor of the potential of charter schools to help the nation's "at risk" education system.[1]

For the public, Shanker's endorsement of an eminently popular idea has complicated our education debate. I should note, first and foremost, the importance of Shanker's leadership. For the education reform movement, a union leader's endorsement of potential change was a significant step. Any praise from a teachers' union for genuine educational reform is the near equivalent of squeezing blood from a stone. But more than a decade since Shanker's speeches on behalf of charter schools, the teachers' unions have been caught in a bind. The movement has spread far beyond what anyone originally imagined.

Some guardians of the status quo believe that charter schools work. They are willing to mouth a few platitudes about the charter movement; yet, at the same time, they go right back to doing everything they can to undermine the spread of accountability, innovation, and results-focused reforms. Often, their opposition can be explained by the fact that charter schools typically exist outside the purview of the teachers' union contract. (In some charter schools, however, teachers may elect to become unionized.)

The hypocritical treatment of the charter school movement, in my opinion, is one of the strongest indictments of teachers' union leadership. Nowhere is this more apparent than in the debate in the fall of 2004 illustrating the reasoning behind my First Law of Union Hypocrisy: that is, the objectors of education reform will ignore all evidence of failure—except in those cases when failure involves charter schools or choice programs. Antireformers abhor rigorous standards for the curricula used in conventional, traditionally run schools. They impede regular measures of student progress and achievement. And they actively challenge any reform that would bring transparency to their own books and political operations. (There are, of course, individual exceptions to this war against accountability.) Yet all this resistance to accountability and to exposing failure disintegrates the moment a study, a story, or a fragment of research comes out that shows a charter school or a choice program lagging in performance.

By the summer of 2004, the AFT had proven once and for all that teachers' unions and charter schools do not mix. It was in August of that year when the AFT released the results in an in-house study based on the National Assessment of Educational Progress (NAEP). After looking at the numbers from what is called The Nation's Report Card, the AFT's researchers declared that charter schools underperformed in comparison to traditional public schools.[2]

For the *New York Times,* the guardian newspaper of a city with thousands of children in failing public schools, this negative finding on charter schools was banner-headline, front-page news. As journalist Diana Jean Schemo put it:

> The first national comparison of test scores among children in charter schools and regular public schools shows charter school students often doing worse than comparable students in regular public schools. The findings, buried in mountains of data the Education Department released without public announcement, dealt a blow to supporters of the charter school movement, including the Bush administration.[3]

The story and the firestorm that followed were startling indicators of the *New York Times'* partisan nature—an all-too-eager partisanship that lent itself to sloppy reporting, and even a basic professional failure by a journalist to challenge her sources. As the facts would bear, not only had the *New York Times* irresponsibly drawn the wrong conclusions from incomplete numbers, the journalist implied that secret and nefarious motives prevented the United States Department of Education from releasing the numbers. Of course, this led to a concatenation of negative publicity in papers across America.

As a supporter of accountability and measuring results, I am never one to back away from uncomfortable findings or brutal facts. To help children, we must hunt, find, and uncover failure. Indeed, as Houston's superintendent and as US secretary of education, I directed my efforts at trying to find meaningful measures of how our schools are performing for the education of our children. Yet, as the *New York Times* story pointed out, for our measures of student performance to be meaningful guides, we must take care to use the information responsibly.

In response to the *Times*, I immediately issued a public statement highlighting one of the cardinal rules for interpreting any study of charter schools: "The *Times* made no distinction between students falling behind and students climbing out of the hole in which they found themselves."[4] Furthermore, I added:

> It is wrong to think of charter schools as a monolith. There are schools for dropouts, schools for students who've been expelled, schools serving the most economically disadvantaged families. Charters are as diverse as the children they educate. In fact, according to the authors of the data the *Times* cites, [*differences between charter and regular public schools in achievement test scores vanish when examined by race or ethnicity*]. It is virtually impossible to come up with a statistically significant result otherwise.[5] (Emphasis added.)

Both the researchers at the American Federation of Teachers and the *Times*'s reporter ignored the warning—*issued by the AFT researchers*—contained in the study's executive summary:

> Because minority student achievement is generally low, it is therefore important to ask whether or not charters' disproportionate enrollment of black (but not Hispanic) students explains the lower achievement of charter schools relative to regular public schools.[6]

The AFT had used precisely this fact—the fact that charter schools were trying to right a well-known wrong in public education—to condemn charter schools. The NAEP study looked at just *150* charter schools. In that tiny sample, 61 percent of the charter school population studied was black. According to the National Center for Education Statistics, slightly more than half of charter school pupils were black, Hispanic, or American Indian in the 1999–2000 academic year; the figure for all public schools was one-third.[7]

In fact, as the AFT executive summary *admits*, but downplays, once you control for race, the apparent lack of charter school performance disappears:

> Compared to their peers in regular public schools, black and Hispanic charter school students scored lower both in math and reading in grade 4, *but the differences were not statistically significant.* The achievement gaps between white and black students and between white and Hispanic students were about the same in charter schools as in regular public schools.[8] (Emphasis added.)

To put the smoke-and-mirrors work of the AFT in perspective, just a day later, three Harvard researchers, William G. Howell, Paul E. Peterson, and Martin R. West, analyzed the NAEP data to draw a conclusion that the AFT had resisted for years: traditionally run schools do not educate minority students as well as private, religious schools:

> Data from the National Assessment of Educational Progress (NAEP), often called the nation's report card, show students in charter schools doing less well than the nationwide public-school average, which includes middle-class students from well-heeled suburbs. Similar results are obtained within selected states.
>
> Big deal. These results could easily indicate nothing other than the simple fact that charter schools are typically asked to serve problematic students in low-performing districts with many poor, minority children.
>
> Indeed, if the AFT believes these findings, it must also concede that

religious schools excel. According to the same NAEP data from which the AFT study is taken, religious schools outperformed the public schools nationwide by nine points, a gap that is as large as the public school-charter school difference AFT is trumpeting.[9]

As secretary of education, I was accustomed to occasionally being a lone voice in the education reform debate. But, in this case, I had company. After the article was published, both the *New York Times* and the American Federation of Teachers experienced the full strength of the education reform movement. Just as they did in the case of the forged memos in the CBS case, the education bloggers and expert analyses from across the political spectrum made swift work of the shoddy journalism and manufactured results.

Objections to the *New York Times* and AFT work came from members of Congress, the *Chicago Tribune*, the *Seattle Times*, the *New York Post*, the *Delaware News-Journal*, the Hoover Institution, and more.

Left-leaning columnist Mickey Kaus called the article a "union-made anti-charter hit."[10] The progressive magazine the *American Prospect* stated that the *New York Times*' front-page treatment of the AFT's presentation of the data was a "bit credulous." The *Prospect* stated that "without statistical controls or any kind of longitudinal study it hardly supports the conclusion that 'Nation's Charter Schools Lagging Behind, US Test Scores Reveal'" reports.[11]

The left-of-center Progressive Policy Institute's Weblog Eduwonk mocked the conclusion embodied in the *New York Times* article:

Of course, it's not that simple. For starters most of the charters are new and so this data is better considered as baseline data rather than some sort of final evaluation. In addition, charters tend to serve the most at-risk and struggling students. These can be difficult variables to operationalize, complicating comparisons with other schools even while holding some demographic factors constant.

Most importantly, though, *when one controls the grade 4 data for race, it turns out there is no statistically significant difference between charter schools and other public schools.* But you'll search in vain in the *Times* story for that context.[12]

So, why did so many of the AFT's claims appear in the *New York Times* story—totally uninvestigated, unchallenged, and unanalyzed? I can only conclude that the *New York Times* was trying to drive the story just as much as the special interest that had provided the study. Contrary to evidence from various states, the *Times'* story tried to maintain the illusion that the AFT supported the charter school movement: "The organization has historically supported charter schools but has produced research in recent years raising doubts about the expansion of charter schools."[13] Yet, as analysis by the Center for Education Reform noted, less than 1 percent of charter schools currently in operation meet the AFT's criteria and receive its support.[14]

What's interesting is that despite some caveats in the AFT summary (which cast doubt on the main thrust of the AFT conclusions) the *New York Times'* interpretation went *beyond* the anticharter claims from the AFT itself. The *New York Times* reporter stated:

Because charter schools are concentrated in cities, often in poor neighborhoods, the researchers also compared urban charters to traditional schools in cities. They looked at low-income children in both settings, and broke down the results by race and ethnicity as well. In virtually all instances, the charter students did worse than their counterparts in regular public schools.[15]

Why would any media outlet interested in the truth be so willing to follow the AFT down this dishonest rabbit hole? Perhaps such zealousness derives from the *Times'* attempt to drive their own agenda in an election year.

It wasn't just a case of the *New York Times* acting as a willing accomplice in the obfuscation of an important debate. For the AFT, hypocrisy was at play too. The partisan leadership of the AFT knew from the previous three decades of the education debate that demographic factors are critical to properly understanding education studies. For years, the defenders of mediocrity have stated that we cannot expect more from public schools because we have so many underprivileged minorities dragging down test results. (Granted, they are not always so direct.) But in trying to determine whether charter schools are helping children, it is important to understand the starting point of academic achievement for many of the children attending charter schools. With nearly a two-to-one margin of minority students in charter schools versus conventional schools, it seems relevant to try to control for that variable.

Yet, the AFT's presentation of the study did not point out that charter schools are attempting to fill the holes in the education system.

Chicago's Democratic mayor Richard Daley called the AFT and the *Times'* criticism of charter schools the result of "bureaucracy fighting new concepts."[16] Daley was hard at work trying to improve the schools of Chicago, and charter schools were critical to reform and to hope. Simply put, Daley believed, "We need new concepts in education."[17] For Daley, burdening schools with "more and more bureaucracy"[18] is the real problem.

JUST WHO DO THE CHARTER SCHOOLS SERVE?

Because charter schools are community schools that are not burdened by bureaucracy, they are better able to cater and tailor their school environment, curriculum, and faculty to the specific needs of the student population. Their program offerings vary widely, which helps to explain their appeal to increasing numbers of parents and students.

Consider for a moment how extraordinary the mission of these schools is—and how greatly they are needed when so many schools are run on a factory model:

- At the Alee Academy in Umatilla, Florida, teachers are giving a second chance to at-risk ninth through twelfth graders who have dropped out of conventional, traditionally run schools. The curriculum focuses on helping students earn their high school diploma by developing vocational skills with the ultimate goal of full-time employment.[19]
- Texas American Youthworks Charter School in Austin doesn't just serve Austin dropouts—the program is designed for teenage parents and kids who have a history of gang and criminal involvement.[20]
- On the other side, BASIS Scottsdale in Arizona offers students an accelerated curriculum to challenge its middle school students. Students take chemistry, physics, and biology—*in the sixth grade.* BASIS focuses on holding students accountable for learning by giving the students comprehensive final exams in every subject. Modeled after demanding colleges, these exams are worth 50 percent of their grades. It should be no surprise that in 2004, BASIS sixth graders scored number one in sixth-grade reading, math, and language arts.[21]
- At North Star Academy in Newark, New Jersey, school lasts eleven months. In the month of July, students only attend in the morning, so that teachers can improve their teaching skills and attend workshops to improve their instruction. Despite the fact that the school selects students by lottery, North Star has made some of the most impressive academic gains in New Jersey. In 2004, students scored twice as high as the district average in language arts, and almost triple the average in math.[22]
- At Next Step Charter School in Washington DC, one third of

the student population is made up of teenage parents. Next Step caters to the needs of the Latino-majority student body, working to build English literacy and to develop critical work skills. In addition, the curriculum is based on the goals students set for themselves—which encourages dropouts to continue with their education whatever their work or family needs might be.[23]

Charter schools also vary greatly by their rules and location. Some states have supportive and welcoming legislation that ensures charter schools operate independently of the traditional education system, protected from local school boards ruled by hostile unions—states such as Arizona, California, and Colorado give charter schools more room to maneuver. Then, there are schools where charter laws have been written in a restrictive manner (often under the influence of teachers' union operatives)—in states such as Maryland, Rhode Island, and Mississippi, charter schools struggle to survive, with just a few able to prosper.

CHARTER STUDIES TO CONSIDER

Now, despite what the *New York Times* and the AFT would have you believe, there is a great deal of evidence that charter schools are working. In 2004, Harvard education economist Caroline Hoxby released the results of her own study that was, by far, the most thorough analysis of charter school research. Based on data she had gathered on 99 percent of students in charter schools, Hoxby found that "charter students were 5 percent more likely to be proficient in reading than their counterparts at the closest public school of a similar racial composition, and they were 3 percent more likely to be proficient in math."[24]

Plenty of other stories also indicate that charter schools are a source of hope for children most in danger of falling behind, or who have already been abandoned by traditional schools. As research that the Center for Education Reform has collected indicates:

> National survey data finds that charter schools serve a disproportionate share of children least prepared and most behind. Over half of charters serve populations where over 40 percent of their students are considered at-risk or previously dropped out.[25]

The early evidence is that these children are learning faster and making up lost ground. It is only a matter of time before they outperform their peers.

Other studies:

- **Arizona** charter elementary school students perform better than their traditional counterparts. The earlier a child is in a charter school, the better he or she achieves, according to a study of sixty thousand students in Arizona.[26]
- **Wisconsin's** charter schools are doing better than traditional schools based on the results of state tests in fourth and eighth grade for two academic years, according to a 2004 study by Dr. John Witte, University of Wisconsin at Madison.[27]
- In **Michigan**, charters showed greater gains than the statewide average in all but one of ten grades and subjects on the 2003 MEAP test.[28]
- Sixty percent of urban charter schools in **Massachusetts** outperformed comparable traditional schools on the 2003 MCAS exams.[29]

Yet these successes—and the fact that charter schools reduce bureaucracy and empower principals and teachers—are precisely the reasons why the teachers' unions have fought hard to destroy the movement.

When the charter school movement first began, the movement was too small to attract adverse attention from teachers' unions. In fact, Al Shanker was an early backer when a few teachers in Minnesota decided to open the first charter school in the country. In the early 1990s, the guardians of mediocrity saw parental choice and options as a real threat to their monopoly. Charter schools were merely an afterthought. But, as the number of charter schools grew—and grew quickly— the teachers' unions turned from contemptuous indifference to outright opposition.

The teachers' unions—politically savvy—are threatened by the popularity of charter schools. Charter schools might loosen the unions' choke hold on education. In charter schools, parents and journalists were able to find a middle ground between the shocking reform possibilities of school vouchers and a continued support for the education system as it stood. Charter schools presented the best of both worlds. By starting up *new* schools, which met *real* needs, charter schools did not appear to be destroying the existing infrastructure of traditionally run schools and compulsory dues collection. So, the teachers' unions were presented with a real dilemma: how to undermine the charter school movement without fully exposing their inexcusable defense of a status quo that desperately called for reform.

In states that lacked charter schools, teachers' unions took one of two positions: fearmongering or domination.

In state after state, the teachers' unions pulled political strings to fund high-priced smear campaigns to undermine charter schools. What follows is clear evidence of this.

Even after **Washington's** state representatives passed charter school legislation, the teachers' unions did not give up. They sought a referendum to eliminate the legislation *against the wishes of many of the rank-and-file school teachers.*[30] By the time the governor of Washington signed the legislation into law, his office had been flooded with calls from teachers who wanted to work at the new charter schools.

Recently, the debate reached a boiling point when the state's most famous citizen jumped into the fray. Nationwide, the Bill and Melinda Gates Foundation had pumped more than $135 million into charter schools. Yet none of this money was benefiting the students in Gates's backyard. Voters rejected charter school initiatives in the 1996 and 2000 elections, thanks largely to union-financed campaigns against them. (In 2000, Gates's fellow Microsoft billionaire, Paul Allen, financed the voter initiative supporting charter schools.[31]) In March 2004, the state legislature passed charter school legislation, which was then overturned with a union-supported voter initiative this past fall.

It's certainly worth noting that time and again, private donors find supporting public education to be a losing proposition. Gates, as Harvard's most famous dropout, would like to support public education, but his savvy business sense tells him supporting traditional public schools, as they stand now, may not be the best, nor the only worthwhile, investment. By any objective standard, Gates's contribution would be good money after bad. But charter schools have a degree of accountability that makes them a much better investment in children, as well as more attractive to private donors.

In **Michigan**, the Detroit Federation of Teachers threatened to file suit against Central Michigan University and other schools that wanted to create new charter schools—*already authorized* by the state legislature. The *Detroit News* noted that teachers did not have a lot to complain about. Teacher salaries were second highest in the nation. Administrators were also paid generously. And yet, nearly half (47 percent) of Detroit's adult population could not read. Despite this evident need for reform, this was not the first time Detroit's teachers' union had declared war on charter schools.[32]

In 2003, entrepreneur Robert Thompson offered $200 million to build fifteen charter schools. But the teachers' union tapped its

THE WAR AGAINST HOPE

political power to force Mayor Kwame Kilpatrick to kill the deed. What compounds this misfortune is the fact that had the city accepted the seed money, charter schools would have received an *additional* $200 million in matching funds. As the *Detroit News* editorialized, "The teacher unions should get out of the way and allow every available option to be exploited to make sure more Detroit school children receive a decent education."[33] The teachers' union in Michigan is now lobbying to keep the cap on charter schools—as well as add new restrictions on who can authorize the founding of new charter schools.[34]

In **Kansas**, the United Teachers of Wichita (UTW) used its influence over the Wichita school board to try to destroy the Edison charter school. In Wichita, the school board supervises charter schools. So, first, the UTW tried to cut off funding to the schools. Then the union filed a lawsuit against the district and withdrew it, only after the district agreed not to open two new charter schools.[35]

In **Minnesota**, the teachers' union sought caps for the number of charter schools allowed in the state. In addition, the union pursued legislation that would allow only school boards to start charter schools, thus putting charter school reformers under the thumb of the same bureaucracy that holds back traditional schools—a bureaucracy controlled by office holders supported by union political money.[36]

In **Tennessee**, a proven charter school, the Knowledge Is Power Program (KIPP), was thwarted in its efforts to open a new school. KIPP is a confederation of forty-five independently operated schools that has been gaining a national reputation for turning even the most troubled students into academic success stories. Even though the Tennessee state board unanimously approved the founding of a KIPP academy, state law allows charter enrollment only for students who attended schools that have been rated as "low-performing" for at least two years. In the Nashville area, three separate schools were failing to meet the state's minimum requirements. But none of these failing schools were *middle* schools, the age group that the KIPP school targets. Thus, the narrow scope of the charter law in the Volunteer State prevented the KIPP academy from opening for the 2004 school year.[37]

"The whole thing is very unfortunate," said executive director of the state board Douglas Wood, reflecting on what had occurred in Tennessee. He added, "The law should focus not on low-performing schools, but on kids who are below proficient."[38] For elected leaders, the threat of being labeled "anti school" by teachers' union money and operatives often creates pressure to write laws such as Tennessee's.

In **California**, basketball star Kevin Johnson returned to his poverty-stricken community to help renew the neighborhood. As part of his effort, Johnson became involved in an initiative to revitalize the failing schools of the largely minority Oak Park, south of the state capitol. When the school board decided to shut down Sacramento High, his alma mater, for continuing its dismal academic performance, Johnson joined reformers in using the Sacramento High campus to build six new, smaller charter schools. The school board approved the plan. Parents and community leaders joined in the cause. UC-Davis volunteered money and educational expertise, and local businesses donated money and materials. Johnson was on the brink of success.[39]

But the California Teachers Association (CTA) hit back hard. The union began to throw up every possible roadblock, including taking the district to court. The CTA insisted that the board and Johnson's charity had not gotten the proper number of signatures from the teachers at the failing campus. State law, driven by union demands, absurdly required that half of a school's teachers must endorse the conversion of a traditional school to a charter school.[40] This, of course, puts the teachers in the way of any meaningful change, at least in the eyes of the union. But the union pressed forward to try to kill the community's plan for improving the school. (And never mind the fact that were the school closed outright and later reopened, parental support was all that the reformers would need.) The unions simply had too much to lose.

In the first trial, the union lawyers lost. So they changed judges. Superior Court judge Trena Burger-Plavan stopped the reforms, saying it was all too fast. Once again, the union lawyers could not win the argument about the right of the school board to close the school, nor could they argue against the fact that the district and community could open a charter school.

Daniel Weintraub, columnist for the *Sacramento Bee*, uncovered another reason the union leadership had broken out the brass knuckles:

> One subtext to all this is that the district's teachers are threatening to strike this fall over a new contract. If the new Sac High is allowed to proceed with non-union teachers, it could well stand as the only school in the city to open on schedule in September. That would give it tons of publicity and potentially weaken the union's position in negotiations with the district.[41]

Thanks to Kevin Johnson, the boys and girls of Sacramento High had new hope. For the unions, there was simply too much to lose if the kids started learning. Unfortunately, these kids' teachers were still paying dues to their local political machine.

In **Ohio**, the Ohio Federation of Teachers (OFT) and Ohio Education Association (OEA) tried to use the courts to shut down all of the state's charter schools. When that failed, the teachers' union threatened to try and pass a statewide referendum to eliminate all 179 existing charter schools if the state legislature didn't stop the opening of new charter schools. In a striking example of how the politically partisan leadership thinks about charter schools, OFT president Tom Mooney said that the moratorium would not apply to the forty-six schools sponsored by public school districts—districts where union money and political machinery could control the district boards that fund and control charter schools.[42]

In state court, the OEA filed a suit claiming that the state's charter schools violate the Fourteenth Amendment—denying due process and equal protection under the law. The union's attack sought to enjoin the state from its current method of funding the charter schools. The OFT also filed two other suits seeking to stop the funding of charter schools.[43]

Meanwhile, union opponents of charter schools opened another front in the war—filing suit in federal court. In May 2001, the OFT, the Ohio School Boards Association, the Ohio League of Women Voters, and the Ohio PTA filed suit. On 21 April 2003, Judge Patrick McGrath of the Franklin County Common Pleas Court dismissed a majority of the allegations and ruled that the Ohio state constitution does allow charter schools to exist and to be funded.[44]

But in late August of 2004, a federal appeals court judge ruled that the federal suit must be heard and that it must be determined if it violates the constitution for charter schools to receive a portion of local property taxes, in addition to state aid.[45] The Ohio Supreme Court heard the case in November 2005.[46]

The grim irony for the struggling charter school movement is that the movement actually means *more money* for local, traditional public school districts. Not only do charter schools tend to serve poor, minority students who are being left behind, but charter schools often get only state and federal support. In Ohio, for instance, the average district receives 48 percent of their revenue from the state, with another 46 percent coming from local tax revenue. Charters do not get that local support and must fend for themselves.[47]

Thus, for the charter movement, the Ohio teachers' unions' law suits were crippling to their efforts to help children. As of the fall of 2004, according to researcher Terry Ryan, charter schools had to raise $1.2 million themselves just to defend against the union with its nearly bottomless coffers of money collected through compulsory teacher-union dues.[48] Ryan concluded grimly:

> There is every reason to expect charter schools will ultimately prevail in both the state and federal suits, but charter school opponents don't necessarily seek or expect judicial victory. Theirs is a war of attrition designed to wear down, fragment, disrupt, confuse and exhaust charter operators, teachers, parents and supporters alike.[49]

What these examples, and many others from around the country, show is the hatred that teachers' unions have for charter schools. While their rhetoric may range from cagey acceptance to outright hysteria, their actions reveal a consistent and implacable opposition to charter school reform.

At their annual convention in 2001, the NEA expanded its guidelines on charter schools. The union stated that charter school teachers should be required to be licensed and certified by the state in the same way as other public school teachers. In addition, the NEA reiterated its commitment to opposing the founding or continued operation of any charter schools that are run by private education-oriented corporations.[50]

Despite these hardball tactics, the popularity of charter schools is soaring. That has led some state affiliates of teachers' unions to reevaluate their tactics. According to the Buckeye Institute for Public Policy Solutions, after a lengthy study, the Pennsylvania State Education Association (PSEA) decided that they could no longer fight charter schools.[51] The internal report stated that "attempts to prevent the granting of charters can have negative public relations consequences."[52] In addition, the report admitted that charter schools "will continue to extend their reach because they provide an expanded range of consumer choices and also provide options for students who are not fitting well into their regular public schools."[53]

The PSEA would instead organize the charter school teachers in order to gain the political power that comes from compulsory union dues.

Of course, organizing teachers at charter schools presents a host of problems for unions—and they know it. First, many teachers in charter schools are quite capable of solving their own problems. They do not need more bureaucracy—whether it is the staid and stuffy administrative kind or the confrontational and frenetic union kind. Second, unions must work hard to convince charter school teachers that they are being abused and need union representation. Charter schools have an average of 240 students, many with far less. This represents a limited payoff for unions. Finally, teachers' unions face the fact that many, many teachers prefer to teach at charter schools. For instance, when the Renaissance Charter School in Boston, Massachusetts, had an opening, more than seven hundred teachers applied to fill one of the thirty-six positions at the school. Similarly, at Marblehead Charter School more than five hundred teachers applied for just seven slots.[54]

CHARTERS: WHAT THE UNION CRITICS MISS

What is interesting about so many studies of charter schools is the focus on the race between charter schools and the factory-model, traditional schools. Critics produce studies trying to prove charter schools don't improve student performance as much as the bureaucratic model. But this misses the point. By their mere existence, charter schools are prompting academic improvement in the traditional public school system. What charter and choice programs both prove is that competition to serve children works. In many researchers' desperation to "prove" choice and charter schools a failure (or simply a less successful alternative), these competitive studies put the focus on how schools perform in achieving the most important bottom line: improving children's lives and opening the doors of opportunity.

One problem with these studies, however, is that the question is not between the brick-and-mortar charter school and the brick-and-mortar public school. The real measure should be the success of the curricula, teaching methods, and teaching staff at these schools. As we have seen, the charter school movement is a highly dynamic movement serving the diverse needs of hundreds of thousands of children. It is critical to keep in mind, however, that charter schools open their doors to children who are being left behind by the factory model. Charter and choice schools exist because public schools have failed in their primary mission. Therefore, charter and choice schools are often taking in children who have more to learn because the traditional model wasn't working for their educational needs.

Of course, some charter schools do fail—much to the glee of political partisans in the teachers' union and antireform movement. But charter school freedom is predicated on their own responsibility. Charter supporters don't look on a single charter school's failure as an indictment of the charter school system. They see it as evidence that the charter school system works. Charter schools can experiment as they like, but they must ultimately get results.

To compare charter schools as a movement against the public school status quo can thus be misleading. Not all charter schools are equal. But the fact that they are answerable, accountable, and must serve the students guarantees that in the long run the right curricula, instruction methods, and teaching expertise will be most efficiently tailored to students. In the current traditional school system, there was little incentive before NCLB for schools to improve or adopt scientifically researched, academically proven curricula. Charters are accountable.

The competition is so powerful that even the modest influence of charter schools raises the bar for the surrounding public schools. Even as charter teachers dismantle the unproven theories and curricular fads of liberal education colleges, time will eventually vindicate charter schools, and their success will translate into opportunity and hope for thousands of children.

THE FUTURE OF THE RESEARCH

This is not the first time these kinds of attacks have been unleashed on charter schools. Nor will they be the last. In these seesaw battles of research and data, the traditional news cycle shows those against school reform working behind the scenes to drive the negative stories. Then reformers try to counter with their own studies, or they attempt to spin the success of charter school reform.

What these debates often miss is the extraordinary conduct of the objectors in the way that they are trying to use proreformers' desire for accountability *against* these reformers.

When a charter school fails or a charter school study doesn't indicate strong student achievement and progress, few critics ask why the defenders of the status quo should care. They resist accountability in almost every aspect of our education system. So, what is one more failure or misstep?

It is sheer hypocrisy for union partisan and antireform operatives to attack charter schools or choice schools. Charter schools and choice founders have agreed to take on the challenge. They have *embraced* accountability. Charter schools in particular have a special onus on them to perform because their contract with the state and the community is that they will get results. As the Progressive Policy Institute noted in the wake of the attack by the AFT and the *New York Times*:

Is every charter school great? Of course not. Are there too many low-performing ones? Yes. However, the solution to that problem is not to do away with charters but rather to ensure that public policies rigorously weed-out the low-performers while not hamstringing the many high performing public charter schools changing the lives of youngsters every day.[55]

When objectors attack charters for negative numbers, they are merely disparaging a group of idealists who put pressure on themselves because they believe that every child should learn. Equally mysterious is the gloating response of teachers' unions that follows the news of a failing charter school or of a charter school founder who has wasted money. (Once again, the hypocrisy gets little attention.)

When a charter is shut down for failing to meet its contract obligations, we should remember this is *good* news. The fact is, this is the way the system is *supposed* to perform. When a school shuts down because it is not helping children achieve, it is a profound reminder that our schools are built to serve children and parents. Their mission isn't their own self-survival; their mission is to perform and achieve results.

Shutting down schools that aren't up to standards raises expectations, and eventually performance, in our entire education system. If we want to put children first, we must put failing schools second. We must first get children help in schools that work before we start wasting students' lives by trying to save a school just for the sake of keeping the bricks-and-mortar operation or spending-and-budget paperwork in circulation or for providing jobs for adults.

The question teachers' unions must ask themselves is: How long can we use the issue of accountability to attack the reformers before the public demands the same results from every public school?

8

VISION FOR THE FUTURE

"We now accept the fact that learning is a lifelong
process of keeping abreast of change. And the most
pressing task is to teach people how to learn."

—Peter Drucker

"It is not necessary to change.
Survival is not mandatory."

—W. Edwards Deming

There are so many special interest groups in education who have much to lose if the current system is reformed. These interest groups have been appallingly blunt about the fact that the welfare of students is less important than their own selfish concerns. They refuse to look in the mirror when faced with irrefutable evidence that their own actions are harming the nation's children and are eager to blame straw men rather than be held accountable.

For years, unions have howled that the failures of the educational system are due to a lack of funding for teachers and schools. If the No Child Left Behind Act has done anything, however, it has proven, once and for all, clearly and unequivocally, that the furor surrounding the question of spending is not just irrelevant to how most schools perform, it is a costly distraction. Some of the highest performing schools and districts have some of the lowest per pupil expenditures. And conversely, some of the worst schools and districts spend huge amounts of money per student, with little to show for it.

As a nation, we have spent more on education nearly every year for the last one hundred years. Additionally, contrary to what the big teachers' unions would have the public believe, No Child Left Behind has provided record spending—spending beyond the wildest imagination of even the most liberal senators and congressmen in previous administrations. Under President Bush, in fact, federal spending on education grew 49 percent in the first four years, more than in the entire administration of Bill Clinton.[1]

Sadly, teachers' unions have used the issue of education spending as a smokescreen to confuse the public, as a political weapon to divide the electorate, and as a red herring to distract the public from desperately needed reforms. Because the spending issue is so important, and because the facts are so often twisted, I believe it is important for reformers to inject into public debate a few relevant statistics on increases in education spending. Actual spending—quantified and made clear to the public—helps show how little bang we get for the taxpayer buck. Furthermore, rather than student-to-teacher ratios, the public should examine teacher-to-administrator ratios. And finally, we need to compare the growth rate in bureaucracies to the growth rate in school funding.

I promise you that these simple statistics will open the public's eyes wide and run directly counter to the misinformation they are currently being subjected to. Though it is clearly dishonest to say that the most important element of a successful school is financial resources, one hears the argument made all the time that money is the solution.

But opponents of meaningful school reform need to keep the

debate about money alive because it diverts attention away from the real question: why do some schools fail and others succeed?

If we are to ensure a better future for America's children, we have to figure out the key determinants of school success. Like most people, when I read a story about a school that works or see that kind of report on TV (or feel it when I visit such a school), I ask, "Why can't we imitate this school?" In those cases where we find successful schools and programs, we should, and can, replicate them. The problem is, success is often the result of innovation; but under the current system, schools have no incentive to innovate, even when they are clearly failing.

That leads me to the second thing that must happen in order to ensure better schools and a better future for our children: schools and educators who fail their students must be held accountable. This lack of accountability, in my view, is the greatest crime in American education.

As a people, we believe that education should provide equality of opportunity for *all* our children. Americans believe that education is not just important for maximizing the potential of every individual child; education is a necessity for our representative form of government. We believe that schools must be improved if we are to be a nation with an educated electorate, a competitive economy, and hope for every child, of any race, who dares to dream the American dream.

American people have become educated about education, thanks in no small part to No Child Left Behind. And as a result, they are loudly calling for change to the current system. The educational status quo and the defenders of mediocrity can try to stall reform and doom another generation of children to narrowed opportunity and handicapped futures. But ultimately, I believe, the reformers will win. They are the future. Public education will get better. The questions are, how much, and how fast?

Parents, voters, and taxpayers have long stated that education should be the top domestic priority for political action. For almost a decade, governors, legislators, and reformers throughout the fifty states have slowly increased accountability measures, raised state standards, and tried to integrate meaningful testing into our public schools. It hasn't been perfect, but even this glacial pace of reform has been too much for the system and its defenders.

What has been most critical—and most threatening to the phalanx of teachers' unions and self-esteem gurus that defend the status quo—has been the steady increase in testing. Objectors of school reform have fought these measures hard, using every type of argument imaginable to try to scuttle and prevent reform. But, like the old Soviet bloc, a little *glasnost* will go a long way. The smallest beams of light on the system will be devastating. As parents and the public realize that it is *their* local school and *their* kids who are falling behind, the system will change. As the "report cards" on local schools come in, information and insight into the school down the street will provide the tipping point for change.

The No Child Left Behind Act is providing that critical information—or *glasnost*, if you will—that will expose and indict the *nomenklatura* in the teachers' unions, those who believe the needs of the bureaucratic rulers should come before the needs of the child, the family, and the citizen.

Everyone—except teachers' unions and their leadership—is beginning to realize that more spending is not the answer. This isn't just coming from conservatives, who have been saying this for years. Some courageous Democrats are saying it too. As Democratic senator Evan Bayh of Indiana acknowledged in 2001, "From now on, we will no longer measure success in terms of how much we spend. Instead we will focus on how much our children learn."[2]

Bayh and twenty-three other House and Senate Democrats wrote to President Bush to support the need for reform. "We agree on the need for reorienting our federal education policy to make it more performance-based, with much greater emphasis on results instead of rules and regulations. We agree on the need for streamlining the federal bureaucracy, providing local districts with more flexibility to decide how best to allocate their federal aid to meet their local priorities, and encouraging principals and teachers to experiment with innovative programs and practices."[3]

The defenders of mediocrity and the special interests, who oppose even the most minute change to the status quo, like to call reformers "enemies of public education." But as the public learns more about the deficiencies and shortcomings of our public schools, it will become more and more clear that the schools cannot change unless special interests get out of the way. And no special interest is more destructive than the teachers' unions, as they oppose nearly every meaningful reform. As support for public schools wavers, the public will seek new outlets and options. Black parents in inner city Cleveland, Milwaukee, and Washington DC are already fed up, and they have turned to school choice, opportunity scholarships, and private help in order to ensure their children attend schools that will give them a leg up in life.

As frustration sets in—especially for poor parents and parents of minority children—the demand for reform will grow exponentially. The question is not if, but when will this pressure hit critical mass. What the special interest and union partisans fail to understand is that No Child Left Behind is their last hope. NCLB is designed to save traditional public schools and to rejuvenate hope in the public school system.

Still, some are frustrated with the many obstacles that block meaningful change. Howard Good, a former school board member in New York State, writing in *Education Week*, stated that "the near-impossibility of true education reform has been documented in a number of studies." Buttressing the point with his own bitter experience, he adds, "Now that I'm off the board and able to think more calmly, it is even clearer to me that the system can't be rehabilitated, only replaced. . . ."[4]

Former NEA and AFT affiliate's officer David Kirkpatrick agrees:

"Ironically, the public school system's wounds are largely self-inflicted. It has repeatedly demonstrated an inability to reform itself. Despite ever-increasing costs, it remains unable to adequately educate low-income and minority students. And countless citizens have experienced firsthand a cool, even antagonistic, response from school boards, educators and teachers' unions when they question the status quo."[5]

Kirkpatrick, a lifelong member of the NEA, points to plenty of hard-core evidence of the public's dissatisfaction. And this isn't the petulance of a few disgruntled parents talking to pollsters. Parents and taxpayers are taking action that is showing up in two trends.

Parents' choice to home school is the first of these indicators of unrest. In 1981 an estimated ten thousand students were being home-schooled. Estimates now run as high as two million. And there are those who say the trend is growing at about 15 percent a year. Most importantly, studies consistently show home-schooled students perform well academically and socially. Prestigious colleges and universities not only willingly accept such students but actively recruit them. This challenges the rhetoric about the necessity for teacher certification. This embarrassment also helps explain the antagonism to home schooling by "professional" teachers.

The second outcome of the nation's disappointment with public schools is, of course, the development of charter schools. There were none in 1991. Today there are nearly three thousand, enrolling more than seven hundred thousand students. Some state charter school laws are extremely weak. Others, in states such as Arizona, California, and Michigan, have resulted in the creation of hundreds of schools in each state. Of course, like countless public schools, some charter schools have problems. Unlike the traditional schools, however, charter schools with serious difficulties are likely to close. Still, their overall record is positive, and some have experienced success matched by few, if any, traditional schools.[6]

It is heartening to see a veteran of the AFT and NEA such as Kirkpatrick confront the brutal facts and see the need for deep, meaningful reform.

In defending the indefensible, teachers' unions are endangering America's schools. As confidence in the system sags because the schools do not improve, the choice will be clear. As one editorial from the *Daily News of Los Angeles* noted in the bitter fights to elect a non-union school board:

> It's either back to the basics with a school board that represents the public and parents, not the players, or it's break up and move forward. It's anything that smashes the status quo.[7]

What Do Parents and the Public Want in the Schools?

My travels as secretary of education have taken me to nearly every state of the union. Throughout America, parents want the same thing: a clean, orderly school environment with a strong culture of learning, where children respect their peers and their teachers, teachers and specialists identify their children's needs quickly, and the curriculum provides a challenging education focused on fundamental skills required for success.

But there is no need to take my word for it. In some of the most comprehensive opinion polling to date, a group called Public Agenda has asked tough questions and sought concrete answers from parents, teachers, education professors, even children.

What parents want isn't complicated. In fact, it is very straightforward. The reason the public and politicians aren't more familiar with the fundamental desires of parents boils down to the personal attacks leveled by demagogues and fueled by the partisan leadership of teachers' unions. According to "First Things First: What Americans Expect from the Public Schools":

- The public and parents want schools to impose tougher standards, and they want teachers to teach basic skills of writing, spelling, math, and science.
- Nearly nine in ten (88 percent) think that schools should raise standards and use graduation exams.
- Three-quarters (75 percent) want schools to stress English, math, and science first.
- Fully 73 percent want schools to take action and kick out persistent troublemakers.
- Over half (52 percent) want schools to demand good work habits from children, teach kids to be on time, and hold children accountable for doing their homework.
- And more than 86 percent of the public want children to learn how to do math without using calculators.[8]

What's amazing is that students know what schools should be doing, too.

Another Public Agenda survey, "Getting By: What American Teenagers Really Think about Their Schools," interviewed 1,300 public and private high school students.

- More than seven out of ten high school students said they would study harder and pay attention more if their schools required them to learn more and only let them graduate after passing rigorous tests.
- Three out of four think diplomas should go *only* to those with a strong command of the English language. Some 79 percent of whites, 71 percent of Hispanics, and 68 percent of blacks support that requirement.

- Fully 94 percent of high school students think they should be learning basic reading, writing, and math skills before graduation.
- Eighty-six percent said that by graduation they should have to learn how to be on time and how to stay disciplined. A solid majority of students (81 percent) believe that one result of twelve years of education should be an appreciation for the value of hard work.
- Nearly eight in ten students said they would also learn more if schools enforced work deadlines, which most believed were lax at best. As one student put it, "You can just glide through. You can copy somebody's homework at the beginning of the period. They practically hand you a diploma."
- Unfortunately, more than 70 percent of students complained about "too many disruptive students." And 80 percent said they could learn more and learn better if problem teens were removed.[9]

Looking at these startling results, Public Agenda's executive director said, "Students are issuing a distress signal, and it's time for us to stop the blame shifting . . . and focus our energies on addressing their plea for order, structure, and moral authority in their lives."[10] Ironically, students are better focused on the mission of our schools than many in the antireform movement are.

If these results—the view from the public on the outside and the view from students on the inside—are correct, as I believe they are, then the potential for implementing meaningful reform is enormous. The demand is there. What we have been lacking for decades is the political will and a mechanism to ensure that reform is fully executed.

But the elite opinions of a few education professors and teachers' union leaders have been fighting to take schools in exactly the opposite direction. They believe our students are taxed by too much testing, too many demands, and too many deadlines. The evidence simply isn't there, though. Teachers are not being forced into dicta-torial positions, pounding kids with too much work. And even if they were, that is a problem that is much more easily remedied than the current tolerance of ignorance. It is better we demand too much of our students and have them fall short, than to demand nothing of them at all.

Until the debate was truly begun by President George W. Bush, American education had all the hallmarks of a losing team in the National Football League. In the NFL, and in business, we have seen that turning around an organization follows a clear, unequivocal path: high expectations and standards, not self-esteem talks and spending, are needed to achieve tangible, meaningful, lasting results.

I am not speaking about theoretical possibilities or airy notions pulled from castles built in the sky. I've seen the future. We have such schools already.

ISLANDS OF EXCELLENCE IN A SEA OF MEDIOCRITY

Perhaps the most amazing examples of how education and public schooling can work is the Knowledge Is Power Program (KIPP) Academy in Oakland, California. KIPP academies have sprung up all over the nation, using an education model that directly communi-cates to children the value and importance of education. Students earn knowledge points each week, based on what they learn and how they study. Students can then trade in those earned points at the school's store to "buy" school supplies and prizes. At the end of each year, students can use the points they've earned all year long to take a school trip to Disneyland. About 70 percent of children go on that trip every year. Just as important, if not more, 30 percent are forced to stay at home because they did not meet the standards and expec-tations of education. KIPP holds students accountable for what they learn and ensures they will contribute to their own educational development and achievement.

What makes the KIPP Academy in Oakland so special is that it was a charter school that existed on the second floor of the traditional public school. On the floor below KIPP, the conventional Oakland public schools operated. Graffiti, rowdy students, discipline problems, and fed-up teachers were the norm. On the second floor, KIPP students from the same low-income neighborhoods quietly walked to class, waited their turn to answer questions from the teacher, and learn, learn, learn.[11]

The school day starts at 7:30 a.m.—sharp—and continues until 5 p.m. As one teacher, Allison Ohle, says, "There are no bells and whistles here, there is nothing crazy that we do. We just work all day."[12]

Students often attend on Saturdays. And every student must attend three additional weeks in the summer. Teachers are available by cell phone, as late as nine every night, to help children.[13]

KIPP's results were among the best in Oakland, an exciting example for the entire state. In the KIPP academy model, every person involved in education is held accountable—from the school's founders, principals, and teachers to parents and individual students.

"None of us can do our job if the rest of us aren't here doing it and that's what makes us different from any other place I've ever taught," adds Ohle. "Everybody is really trucking everyday to make it happen."[14]

Those teachers who transform the school into an orderly learning environment ideal for growing and inquisitive minds work harder than their traditionally run public school counterparts. But, as teachers in public charter schools, their schools experience less bureaucracy, and they are rewarded for their hard work with salaries that are 15 to 20 percent higher than the average public school teachers. In addition, the very best of the best can earn $10,000 bonuses for outstanding achievement.[15]

Oakland's KIPP academy was one of those successes I saw everyday. It is a story for the whole nation. In the Bay Area of Northern California, KIPP has five middle schools. And the good news is that in 2004, the city-run public school sitting just below KIPP was closed down. The waiting list for KIPP was reduced because KIPP took over the first floor and expanded that culture of learning to a whole new set of public school students. All over this nation there are schools and teachers showing that the protectors of the status quo's excuses are nothing but excuses, spread by partisan teachers' unions who abhor accountability that focuses on the needs of children.

KIPP is only one such success.

But the guardians of the status quo don't want to discuss these successes. Just as they are unwilling to confront the brutal facts, so too are they unwilling to embrace the brilliant, ingenious, and disciplined success stories. To discuss these success stories would require teachers' unions and their politically partisan leadership to face the reality that money isn't the issue; it's a distraction. Education is the most eminently human of all pursuits, and it requires human excellence, achievement, and mutual respect to ensure knowledge, culture, and civilization are imparted to the next generation.

In Robbins, Illinois, near Chicago, Childs Elementary is another terrific example where it is teachers, curricula, and respectful students that provide the key to learning. Childs is made up of all those kids that the keepers of mediocrity say must wait until funding reaches a level acceptable for the special interests of Washington: 93 percent of the student body come from low-income homes, 96 percent are African-American, and just more than a quarter of the student body move in or out during the school year.[16]

Yet this tiny little school, cordoned off from the streets by rough, chain-link fences, performs magnificently: more than 70 percent of the schools' third graders met or exceeded the Illinois Standards Achievement Tests.[17]

Child Elementary's constant reinforcement of good behavior, citizenship, and rigorous standards help children understand that they are part of a culture of learning.

Children arriving at 8:30 in the morning are greeted by a teacher at the front desk who gives them a handshake, a high five, or a hug. Those who are late have to stay after school.

The curriculum at Childs is focused on the basics: phonics in reading, drills in math to master material, and all the mechanics of clear and concise, as well as creative, writing. As one newspaper put it:

> Kindergartners will be taught to tell stories to their teacher in a paragraph format so they begin to understand the structure of language. Each year, teachers build on that until the pupils are writing full compositions on the computer. Children participate in an accelerated reading program that allows the pupil to select and be tested on a book matched to his reading level.[18]

The powerhouse behind the positive culture at Childs is Principal Louise Dennis—a veteran of public education for more than three decades. Mayor of Robbins, Dr. Irene Brodie, put it thus: "[Principal Dennis] says, 'My kids can do this.' And her teachers exude that type of disposition, too."[19] Louise does her best to keep her best teachers, and jealously defends the belief that every child can learn. Louise also works to ensure that parents feel welcome in her school and part of the process. As anyone who has visited a school like Childs knows, it is a special place where dedication is seen in every room, hallway, and corner of the school. Our challenge is to build a school system that can reward such dedication and make it an example for the rest of the nation.

Inner city students in Boston are having their lives changed by the teachers and staff at University Campus School in Worcester, Massachusetts. Three out of four students at University Campus are eligible for subsidized lunches—a key indicator of poverty. And the student population is selected by lottery. But this school produces results. In 2002, while I was secretary of education, and critics were decrying high standards, testing, and high expectations for kids, University Campus School was proving it could be done. At University Campus School 100 percent of its tenth graders succeeded in passing the statewide tests with an advanced or proficient score. Teacher attendance and student attendance are nearly 100 percent.[20]

How does the school do it? The program works because teachers and students are dedicated to testing to find weaknesses and are committed to fixing the areas of weakness. Before the school year begins in September, incoming seventh graders spend the month of August in an intensive reading course. They take diagnostic tests and review remedial phonics to sharpen their skills. School doesn't let out early: students attend until 4:00 p.m. every day—with kids and teachers often attending ninety-minute classes in order to give more time for learning.[21] Like so many schools, the principal has the autonomy and authority to use flexibility to find innovative solutions. On Wednesday mornings, part-time art and music teachers come to University Campus to teach. Meanwhile, the teachers and faculty are able to meet to work together on common problems. However, not every teacher has what it takes to teach at University Campus. Teachers are available all day long, even after school hours, to help children. They are expected to do whatever it takes to ensure every child learns. These demands sometimes mean that University Campus School does not get any job applications from any other teachers in the Worcester area. At this school, kids aren't the only ones to be held to high expectations.[22] What is beyond argument is that by demanding more from everyone in the learning environment, University Campus School gets results. Such success deserves to be emulated.

We have to learn to look for success and ask what curricula and techniques are working.

- Education Trust found 336 schools in twenty-one states that serve mostly poor populations and produce high achievement.[23]
- The study concluded, "While no single instructional technique, no particular textbook, no curriculum could be credited with producing these schools' gains, one dominant theme did emerge from the survey. All of these schools are unusually focused on high academic expectations for their students."[24]
- The Pacific Research Institute in California found high-achieving, high-performing schools in high-poverty districts: "In interviewing the principals and observing classroom practices, the authors found that most of the schools used direct-instruction methods."[25] As they described the methods preferred by outstanding leader-principals: "Direct instruction is characterized, generally, by teaching in small, logically sequential steps with student practice after each step, guiding students after initial practice, and ensuring that all students experience a high level of successful practice." In addition, the most effective teaching materials provided teachers with instructions "for monitoring and assessing student progress, and for providing immediate feedback to students. Students are tested frequently in order to monitor their progress."[26]

Success is not an accident. Inglewood Unified School District is a high-poverty area neighboring Los Angeles Unified School District (LAUSD). Despite being much smaller than LAUSD, Inglewood has five schools that make the PRI's high-performing, high-poverty list— more than LAUSD. Inglewood focuses on direct instruction and proven instruction methods.

Bennett-Kew Elementary School scores nine out of ten on California's Academic Performance Index, even though 100 percent of its students are in free or reduced-price lunch programs and 34 percent are learning English. Bennett-Kew's students consistently meet and beat the national averages in math and reading—despite the fact that 18–20 percent of the faculty are not credentialed and are teaching under emergency certificates. That's a testimony to research-backed methods.[27]

These schools are just a few of the possibilities. Thousands of schools like these change lives everyday. Our problem is that the teachers' union money and leadership distract and confound what should be the real debate: How do we imitate these schools? How do we implement the best curricula? Why can't every school do this?

The possibilities for change are endless. No child should be tied to a school that is failing him or her. We must repent of the most grievous sin of insisting that a child must continue to attend a school that is failing such a child. As a matter of equality under the law, parents should be free to select a school that best meets their child's needs— whether it's a private or public school; a high-tech cyber-school; a remedial program for pregnant teens; a home school; or a giant magnet school. The future will include a complete matrix of education-delivery systems, each and every one designed, and judged, by how it meets the learning needs, disabilities, and potential of the student.[28]

SURRENDERING WITHOUT A FIGHT

Of course, this promising future and these stories of success hinge on accepting the revolutionary belief that schools are meant to serve children—each of whom can learn and deserves to learn.

In nearly every instance of failure, the faculty, the district, and anti-education reformers appear to secretly believe that some kids just can't learn. They believe discipline is pointless. They believe standards are useless and unfair. They believe that accountability unfairly harms teachers.

Occasionally, this ugly truth surfaces.

In the spring of 2002, as I spread the message of No Child Left Behind and the president's belief that every child could learn and achieve, the grumblings of the antireform group turned from resistance to reform to outright ridicule of the moral vision of education.

For instance, David Finley, writing in the *Arizona Republic*, asserted that "educators know the truth but are afraid to say it: All children cannot learn."[29] He claimed that the landmark education reforms of No Child Left Behind were an example of an emperor with no clothes and a "Band-Aid on a headache."[30]

Finley's criticisms were all the more shocking because he was a school principal. Before he gave up the fight and accepted defeat, he should have considered the consequences that follow from his controversial statement. Such a comment fosters a defeatist attitude that shifts blame from those educators responsible for the status quo. This view eventually becomes self-limiting and self-fulfilling. It was no surprise to me, then, that with a little research I found that the students at his Webster Elementary in Mesa were routinely being left behind because of a substandard education. Finley's negative attitudes were pervasive and destructive to the mission of our schools. Just as a principal's vision, leadership, and determination can create an atmosphere of ambitious optimism that seeks to help every child learn, so too a belief that education is simply beyond some kids will create an atmosphere of sullen pessimism, excuses, and failure.

Finley's own Webster Elementary School provided data that might seem to support his position. Seventy-four percent of students in the racially diverse school qualified for the federal government's free or reduced-price lunch program. Less than one in three of Webster third graders met or exceeded state standards in math. And just over half (52 percent) are meeting minimum expectations for reading.[31]

But before readers get too down, consider a rising star in Mesa just across town from Webster: Lincoln Elementary School.

Lincoln's students were even more impoverished than those at Mesa: 87 percent of the mostly Hispanic student body qualified for free or reduced-price lunches. But at Lincoln, the faculty was getting real results. For the previous three years, scores consistently rose in nearly every category of reading, writing, and math.[32] Particularly good news: nearly three-quarters (73 percent) of Lincoln students met Arizona's rigorous math standards. And 68 percent met the state reading requirements.[33]

Granted, Lincoln still has room for improvement. But the results show just what is possible when education leaders focus on high expectations, a good curriculum, and proven teaching methods.

Every parent knows that few things are more important to a child's future than expectations—high expectations, consistent standards, and individual education all play a crucial role in equipping boys and girls for a prosperous and responsible life in a free society.

Thus, when someone such as Finley dismisses children's futures with the assertion that some children are just hard-luck cases, it is important we stand up and shout, "Wrong!"

If you believe that some children are just going to fall through the cracks, then you will have no problem with our schools. You might, as a protector of mediocrity, instead choose to focus on how much is spent—always postponing helpful reforms because you can always say there is never enough money in the schools.

But, if you believe every child can learn, then you are going to look at our lagging education system and demand immediate action. You will demand meaningful accountability, you will set higher expectations, you will seek information on how every child is doing, and you will want to ensure every taxpayer dollar is spent wisely on one clear objective: raising every child's academic achievement.

This is what President Bush, both parties in Congress, and the American people believe. They believe that justice and equality under the law demand *every* child receive the best education possible. No child's future should be darkened by ignorance, poor teaching techniques, or members of the status quo who say reform isn't possible.

Our nation made a bold commitment in No Child Left Behind. It set a worthy goal: improving every school and giving every child a chance.

When faced with an "underperforming" school, we should not react as Finley does and shrug our shoulders and say, "Does it bother me? Not in the least."

We must build a public education system that can focus on the positive and create reform using proven principles. We must talk about what works and how to emulate those schools that are successfully educating those disadvantaged children who need the basic skills and knowledge to build a better future. We should say, "It can be done."

9

WHAT WE MUST DO

Any institution "degenerates into mediocrity
and malperformance if it is not clearly
accountable to someone for results."[1]

—Peter Drucker

What does the future hold for our public schools? After my four years as the US secretary of education (and as this book attests), it is tempting to look at the future and lose hope, recognizing the history of failures that mark the gravestones of past reform efforts. The moderate, commonsensical No Child Left Behind Act continues to be savaged, despite its modest accountability requirements and record levels of spending. Even in the face of growing competition, I have seen firsthand those who would sacrifice the future of millions of children to maintain their elite positions and stranglehold on political power.

The brutal fact that we must all recognize is that the teachers' unions have little to zero incentive to change. Their power and their desire for control make it unlikely that they will back even the most moderate efforts to bring accountability and results to our schools. In their eyes, we have to remake government, society, families, and our communities before we can expect children to learn. This is just one of the many reasons they seek to increase the power of government and bureaucracy instead of focusing on schools.

But I have also seen ample reason for hope.

In the fall of 2004, I traveled to bring President Bush's message of hope and reform directly to the mostly black residents of our nation's public housing. In particular, I remember one stop in Seattle, appearing before an animated crowd where it seemed more than one-third of the audience had NEA buttons on. As I discussed in the last chapter, the state of Washington has one of the most active and partisan branches of the NEA. The Washington Education Association, for more than a decade, has stopped or slowed almost every meaningful education reform in the Evergreen State.

There I was in Seattle's Holly Park Community Center, in front of one of the toughest groups of union activists in the country. Or so I thought. I spoke briefly about the president's hopes for further reform and his efforts to build a society where black families had their own homes, college savings, and investments. Then I switched over to the subject of education and what the president had done. At first, the audience was restless. They obviously disagreed with the idea that the president was working to improve education. So, at that point I decided to dispense with the pleasantries. I took off my jacket, walked away from the podium, and walked right into the audience to take their questions.

In the course of the next hour, I saw firsthand exactly which myths and which propaganda claims had made their way from Washington DC to this local community in Seattle, Washington. I had heard it all before: The president was not spending enough. He was shortchanging education. He was forcing testing on the states. And so on. And in that hour of discussion, I addressed every one of the teachers' questions. I described the record spending on education and the president's belief that every child can learn. I discussed the importance of specific measures and accountability. As the dialogue continued, the questions became less antagonistic and began to take on an air of earnest respect. I realized that these teachers had never heard the truth. They were so busy working hard to teach their students that they never had the time to stop and think; they believed their union was open and honest about the education debate raging in America. What they eventually came to realize that day was that the president's reforms and the No Child Left Behind Act were in fact sincere, moderate, and well thought out.

At the end of this simple question-and-answer session, I gave my closing remarks—thanking them for doing the real work of education and thanking them for their role in improving education. As soon as I was done, I was mobbed. These teachers, wearing giant buttons in support of the NEA, were hugging and thanking *me*. They were elated with the direct presentation of the facts. And more than one apologized for not looking more closely at the law and instead relying on their union bulletins for information about the law.

It was then and there, after four years of seeing the power of the teachers' unions undermine reform, that I saw the most compelling evidence that we will win. I realized there was good reason to hope that we can improve our nation's schools. Time is on the side of reformers, because as our message and the facts get out, teachers will realize that teachers' unions do not stand for teachers or for schools. They stand for themselves and for their own control of the education system.

As more and more teachers, principals, parents, and political leaders see the buds of reform flower, the teachers' unions will become more and more desperate. As that one day in Seattle showed hundreds of committed teachers, their union cannot be trusted. We may not agree on every detail, but the teachers' unions cannot forever sustain the myth that education reformers are out to destroy the future of children. As their smear tactics are proven to be lies, the chances for meaningful and united reform will increase.

In addition, our reform efforts will be strengthened by the growing imperative for immediate and consequential reform. When challenged—whether it is a terrorist attack, totalitarian expansion, or public corruption—the American public responds.

We are facing a significant challenge. As Richard Florida writes in *The Flight of the Creative Class*:

The United States is now facing its greatest challenge since the dawn of the Industrial Revolution. This challenge has little to do with business costs and even less with manufacturing prowess. And no, the main competitive threats are not China or India. Our country for generations known around the world as the land of opportunity and innovation—may well be on the verge of losing its creative competitive edge.[2]

Students from other countries have been coming to our colleges and universities in large numbers, studying such intense subjects as the sciences, and end up staying in our country. But because of our national security concerns, fewer such students are coming now. So, how will we make up for that loss of brainpower?

We must become more conscious of a growing deficiency in trained scientists and mathematicians in America. Other countries are producing graduates in the hard sciences and mathematics at a staggering rate. For example, India now produces eighty two thousand engineering graduates a year, whereas we only produce sixty thousand.[3] And that American figure is dropping rapidly. From 1985 to 2000, graduation rates for engineers decreased by 23 percent among American college students. The American Society for Engineering Education has released a report, "Engineering in the K-12 Classroom: An Analysis of Current Practices and Guidelines for the Future," which reveals that 88 percent of teachers believe that engineering is important, but only 30 percent of teachers feel that many of their students could succeed as engineers.[4]

The most recent issue of *Inside Higher Education* observes: "The numbers are bleak and—for anyone who cares about the vibrancy of the American economy or the importance of an educated citizenry—deeply worrisome: the United States has fallen to 17th in the world in high school graduation rates and 7th in college-going rates, and is the only industrialized country whose rates are falling. And perhaps most troubling of all, the rates are lowest among those segments of the American populace that are growing the fastest."[5]

The single greatest action we can take to prepare for the twenty-first century is to transform our schools—to make good schools into outstanding schools. We must prepare our students for a global service economy that needs "knowledge workers."

As I look to the future, I see a renewed education system. To get there I believe we need only do a few things:

First, reformers must be bold. As the bipartisan changes of No Child Left Behind show, teachers' unions are trapped by their control of the education system. They are forced to oppose all change. They cannot support any meaningful reform. If every reform is opposed, even one as commonsensical as NCLB, then we might as well advocate any and every bold idea that promises to put power in the hands of parents and focus attention on the needs of the student.

Second, we must continue to open up every aspect of the education system to greater scrutiny. Openness is not a measure of distrust. It is a measure of our commitment to seeing that every child is educated. We must open up the books of teachers' unions. (Or more importantly, challenge the political leadership of teachers' unions to open up their books.) Our political leaders need to track how teachers' union money is being spent. We must also open up our schools to public accountability by supporting meaningful testing and the measuring of results. There isn't a single sector of American society beyond accountability when it comes to public safety, welfare, or trust—everything except our traditionally run schools.

Third, we must make parental and community involvement as

much a part of the education debate as we make the importance of money. We need to provide parents with a sense of importance and control in the education of their children. They must understand that not only are they their child's first educator, they are also part of the accountability system for their local schools. Charters and school choice both give parents a reason to get involved. America is built on the revolutionary premise that freedom and responsibility, together, strengthen each individual and allow our dreams to soar.

Fourth, we must focus on success. Too often our education debates focus on the failures and shortcomings in our education system. We must transform this thinking. Once we believe that every child can learn, we can begin to search for those schools that are succeeding in educating children, especially against the odds. We must challenge those who say it cannot be done with the stories of teachers and schools that show, against all odds, it can be done.

Fifth, we must debate curricula and instructional methods. As the intense debate over reading instructional methods (whole language vs. phonics) has shown, when educators back unproven and untested ideas, a child's chances of learning can be crippled. As our debate about education becomes more national and testing shows what works, we must track down and defend methods of those schools showing that systematic instruction works. We must oppose the absurd notion that tests undermine education. We must remind our fellow citizens how quality control and testing are a part of every innovation and success in human achievement. Even artists and writers take time to evaluate their works to improve their methods and their techniques.

Perhaps this is one area where union political leadership might be able to help. Teachers' unions operate as special interests—seeking to expand power and to take control over schools. Curriculum is traditionally not as lucrative an arena for the pursuit of power. If unions were interested in teachers' well-being in the classroom and not just their own political self-interest, teachers' unions would have enthusiastically supported the provisions of No Child Left Behind and other reforms that help ensure that curricula is scientifically proven before being introduced into classrooms. More than teachers, when curricula is ineffective and based on little more than faddish, politically correct theories of pedagogy, students are the only ones who really suffer.

Teachers and students both lose. In a 1997 essay for the AFT, President Sandra Feldman stated:

> There are many reasons why schools fail. Poor leadership is one of them, and a shortage of qualified teachers is another. Often administrators have settled for weak, watered-down curricula instead of adopting solid, proven programs, and they are unwilling or unable to maintain school discipline. And often there is an unconscionable lack of books and supplies—a sure sign of terrible management, even when resources are scarce. But if we shut down one of these schools—and do it right—the school can come back.[6]

Sixth, we must constantly find ways to convince teachers that their unions do not represent them and that, when unfettered by unions, they are the path to improving education. This means our local school board members and reform-oriented parents must get more involved in directing teachers to literature and Web sites that show the facts. The NEA and AFT spend millions of dollars propagandizing to their members. But no amount can obscure the truth. A single fact-filled article or meeting, like the one in Seattle, can transform a teacher's perceptions about what's at stake in our education debates.

To achieve these changes, we must demand that every segment of American society get involved.

Parents—Parents are our most important allies in determining and setting a culture of learning in schools. Schools must undergo a shift in attitude toward parents' role in education. Administrators, teachers, and school board members should invite parents to participate in meaningful ways, welcome their help, and encourage them to see for themselves what goes on in our schools. Parents would then truly see how necessary their support is for teachers in classrooms. Just one child can be amazingly disruptive for a teacher challenged with reaching an entire class of students, each with differing abilities and skills. By locking parents out of the schools, our worst problems will continue unabated, while the least supportive parents continue to undermine teachers' authority. By involving parents in their children's education, we can rebuild neighborhood schools, as well as put community pressure on those parents who do not guide or discipline their troubled little ones.

School boards—Local school boards are where most of the decisions in education are made. Of all the various governmental entities that influence the quality of the school district, no organization rivals the school boards' power. This is where almost all of the big decisions are made. This is where a community determines the quality and competitiveness of its schools. The school board is the public face of the school system. It hires the superintendents and other school administrators. It sets the policies for hiring principals and teachers. It sets achievement standards, educational policy, and disciplinary guidelines. It makes safety decisions, provides building maintenance, and establishes dietary requirements. In some jurisdictions, it even sets tax rates. The local school boards are running a gigantic operation, with thousands of employees, tens of thousands of students, and a fleet of buses. They have governance of a vast array of school buildings and athletic facilities. The local school board is the center of power in our schools. And if our schools are to be transformed, we must make these school boards better, wiser, and more representative. School board elections, in many ways, determine our future. We need organizations to help train and arm candidates. Such citizen-oriented, reform-minded organizations must identify and recruit potential candidates, and then provide them with information ranging from how to be a candidate and meet financial and political deadlines to how to get informed about curricula and contracts at the local level.

I am hopeful that we can encourage more people experienced in business, military work, and nonprofit involvement to run for the school board. I would like to see those with experience running large companies or other enterprises share their experience and contribute to operating something as large as a school district. As I have observed earlier, many current school board members do not have this kind of experience.

State School Chiefs—State school chiefs, who lead departments of elementary and secondary education in each state, must have the courage to speak out for accountability and testing and promote their importance for ensuring that every child learns. Most school superintendents have some education establishment connections, and many are supported by the teachers' unions. This gives these state school chiefs a unique position by which to take on the role of leadership. Just as the staunchly anticommunist President Nixon was able to go to China to establish ties to counterbalance the Soviet Union, state school chiefs are in a position to work with parents, community leaders, and charter and choice advocates to embrace their desire to see every child learn. We need experiments and ideas so we can build more efficient schools for delivering what every child deserves: a world-class education.

Think Tanks—For the last twenty years, America's think tanks have taken a leading role in equipping political leaders and politically active citizens with information about what is actually going on in education. Organizations, such as the Cato Institute and the Heritage Foundation, have effectively demolished the idea that government-run schools do not get enough money. But we need to develop state resources and turn our attention to the details of what goes on at the local level, especially in school boards. We need organizations that will train and arm parents and citizens to get involved.

Higher Education—Our universities have been forced to take up a lot of the slack for the shortcomings and failures of our public schools. Leaders at this level must begin to ask tough questions of local leaders, such as those regarding why so many students (in some cases more than half of incoming freshmen) require remedial reading, writing, and mathematics courses. Such pressure could help open up debate and force positive change. Universities must also consider rewarding, with scholarships, those who choose the hard sciences and engineering. By going into our poorest performing schools at early ages and offering to support students who stay on track, universities could provide a dream and an inspiration to those in our poorest neighborhoods, those who often see music, entertainment, athletics—and when those fail—crime and illegal drug sales as their only options for a chance at a career.

Perhaps most importantly, colleges who specialize in training educators must abandon the politically correct, psychologically soft belief that curricula should not be challenging and that homework is somehow destructive. For too long, colleges of education and other pedagogical researchers have supported the subjectivist methods of qualitative research, as opposed to the more solid and scientific methods of quantitative research. In an age when improvement is best founded on measurement, evaluation, and quality management, we should be moving in the direction of raising the bar on the curricula being used in our schools. Just as America's economy adapted and competed in the 1990s by abandoning sluggish factory models, so too must our schools become more focused and more efficient in tailoring proven curricula to meet the needs of students.

Journalists—The Fourth Estate plays a powerful role in our democratic way of life. Too often, education beats are considered entry-level jobs from which the best journalists rise to cover politics and foreign policy. But education debates and policy discussions are among the most complex in the public arena. To improve our schools, we need to reward not just the best teachers in the classroom but the best reporters covering education. Education reporters need to learn to view the education arena as both a labor beat and a culture beat, investigating everything from the way contracts undermine excellence and performance pay to how the curriculum in the classroom affects (or undermines) student achievement. In addition, as we struggle to build a more transparent and open education accountability structure, we need journalists skilled in forensic accounting and those with a nose to follow the money. The public knows far too little about how the system covers up copious amounts of information on spending inside and outside the classroom.

Congress—Congress must not take on the role of creating more programs or managing an avalanche of frivolous spending. Their role must mirror the positive, bipartisan reforms of the welfare system under President Clinton in the 1990s. We must recognize that free money without accountability undermines precisely those people it is intended to help. It is our duty to encourage state and local leaders to manage money wisely, as well as demand results from those receiving taxpayer dollars. Our national economy and global leadership are threatened by the collision of noncompetitive schools in a hyper-competitive expansion of free markets. If our schools do not adapt, we will not adapt. This means we must consider legislation that tracks whether federal dollars are making it into the classroom, and we must return to the intent of Title I funding for disadvantaged students. We must attach money not to brick-and-mortar schools; it must be attached to the individual children schools are supposed to be serving with that money. Complicated formulas may create jobs in Washington, but they do not translate into accountability, transparency, or higher pay for our best teachers. Congress must use the reforms of No Child Left Behind and watch closely for how these first reforms play out, at least before expanding into irrelevant areas of ever-higher spending.

Remember, transformation in terms of American education isn't just possible—it is inevitable. The question is what will be the cost, in terms of lives and dreams lost, if our education establishment resists the rigorous self-scrutiny and difficult decisions necessary to transform schools into places where every child receives an equal opportunity to learn.

Around the world, our economic competitors have proven that education reform works. With all the opportunities and interest in this nation, we can transform public education if our teachers' unions would join, instead of oppose, the building of a new, more accountable, transparent, and student-focused system.

We have witnessed the same results in other countries that have made education a centerpiece of their national policy: Ireland, Finland, Norway, Great Britain, Bulgaria, the Czech Republic, Japan, Singapore, and China. These otherwise politically and economically diverse countries all have two things in common: they have students who are very competitive worldwide, and they have made education a pivotal priority.

Take just a few examples: Twenty years ago, Ireland was among the poorest nations in Europe, with its own people as a principal export. Now, the Irish economy is among the strongest in the world, and Irish immigrants are coming back home to good jobs and a bright future.

In an article for the *Washington Post*, journalist Robert Kaiser investigated the Finnish educational system. In that country, which has one of the finest educational systems in the world, students have very high achievement. Why? Because the Finns decided that their greatest resource was their own people and that a superbly educated country could compete better with bigger, wealthier countries.

One educator explained, "The development of Finland has come through investing in the education system." As we consider our own educational future, we must remember that to "invest" doesn't necessarily mean more spending. Rather, we must spend wisely. Our nation's teachers' unions and politicians of both parties must soon confront the brutal fact that the public will soon confront. As more information flows out of our schools exposing the achievement gap and our meager international performance, parents and citizens will ask why. Citizens will soon recognize that federal spending levels on elementary and secondary education from 1965 to the present are not enough. After thirty-five years, state, local, and federal spending has skyrocketed—totaling in excess of a trillion dollars and outstripping most of our international competitors. Yet test scores were roughly the same and performance was lackluster.

Money by itself is obviously not the answer. Investment and alternative incentives are. Effective transformation demands we find the best way to direct taxpayer funds to ideas that have been proven to work; whether it is a traditionally run school, an innovative charter, or a charity-based private school, we must be reaching out to hearts as well as minds.

Fortunately, we have taken brave, if modest, steps down the road of transformation. The citizen coalitions of reform—from concerned parents and business leaders to community activists and elected leaders—are becoming more aware and better organized. And the ideas and principles behind No Child Left Behind are already beginning to bear the fruits of meaningful reform. That means we are changing children's lives for the better.

I had barely left the Education Department before the numbers began to roll in—numbers that vindicated everything I had begun to work for in Houston and in Washington DC.

In July, the National Center for Education Statistics released the first testing since the passage of the No Child Left Behind Act. The National Assessment of Educational Progress showed:

- Nine-year-olds posted the best scores in reading and math in the history of the NAEP report.
- Thirteen-year-olds earned the highest math scores the test has ever recorded.
- Reading and math scores for African-American nine-year-olds reached their highest levels in the history of the test, with reading scores up 14 points and math scores up 13 points in the past five years.
- The gap in reading between white and African-American nine-year-olds was the smallest it had been since testing began.[7]

The battery of editorials and opinion articles I read in the quiet of my private office differed greatly from the scorching criticism I received when I criticized the tactics of the National Education Association and teachers' unions. They were positive reviews—and our teachers and educators and students deserve the praise:

- As *USA Today* put, "Oddly, you heard the sound of one hand clapping last week as the Education Department released national data showing dramatic narrowing of racial learning gaps among elementary and middle school students. The news deserved ringing applause. Rarely can education trends, good or bad, be described as 'dramatic' because they tend to play out at glacial speeds. But the progress 9-year-olds are making in the National Assessment of Educational Progress, the nation's premier sampling of student achievement, qualified as dramatic."[8]
- The *Arizona Republic* noted that "few news stories are as uplifting as those that report improvements in the fruits of education, and the recent results of the National Assessment of Educational Progress bear some ripe, sweet fruit indeed."[9]
- William L. Taylor, chair of the Citizens' Commission on Civil Rights and vice chair of the Leadership Conference on Civil

Rights, called the results "good news for public education and children of color." Taylor's support, speaking for an umbrella group of 180 of the nation's civil rights organizations, is exactly what the political leadership of teachers' unions and the Democrat Party fear: "It may be time for all of us to celebrate this genuinely good news, take a deep breath, and see what we can learn that will inform future efforts."[10]

- The *Virginian-Pilot* summarized most of the coverage: "'Outstanding.' 'Tremendously hopeful news.' Press reports hailing progress by elementary students on a test dubbed 'The Nation's Report Card' aren't hyperbole."[11]

The increase in NAEP scores reflected the focus of reformers: the biggest gains came from states that raised standards with the same high expectations and accountability built into NCLB—with the largest gains flowing from improved education in the South. States such as Texas, North Carolina, Virginia, and Colorado have long been leading the charge with state standards, testing, and improved curricula focused on the basics. I believe these NAEP results are just the beginning of the evidence of what works.

This is not to say that No Child Left Behind has solved everything. There is much more work to do: Reformers must continue to drive new accountability measures, put solid curricula in our classrooms, find new ways to reward our best teachers, and build schools that emulate success in other high-performing schools. The most important thing to do in the interim is to ensure that kids trapped in failing schools find a way out to better schools. For me, and millions of other Americans, saving such children is a matter of fundamental justice, not just good public policy.

After seven decades of living on this earth, and seeing all the change possible in America—from growing up in segregated schools to working as a Cabinet officer for one of our nation's finest presidents—I believe there is no limit to America's promise and potential. This nation's shared belief in freedom, and our continuing trust in the God-given talent of every citizen, has the power to transform America for the better. In the coming years, as we embrace the high ideals worthy of our nation—that *every* child *can* learn—these ideals will change what we expect and demand of our schools, our children, and all those involved in education. I am confident that these heartfelt beliefs will lead to decisive and far-reaching moral action—moral action that will bring hope to millions of American children and a brighter and more equitable future for all.

10

REASONS FOR HOPE

"Our persistent education crisis shows that we have
reached the limits of our traditional model of education.
Given our present and foreseeable demographic,
economic, social, and education circumstances,
we can expect neither greater efficiency nor more
equity from our [present] education system."[1]

—Albert Shanker

In closing this book, I want to make one point perfectly clear: I have abundant faith in the teachers of this nation. To be sure, there are teachers who are in this work for the wrong reasons, and some who should probably pursue other careers. But I am sure that these are the exceptions rather than the rule. Most teachers, I believe, are heroes. Day in and day out, in schools big and small all across the United States, teachers are working very hard to educate and inspire the children who come through their classroom door. The challenges they face can be enormous. For many of them, work extends far beyond the confines of the school building and the school day, and far beyond what their training prepared them to do. But still they persevere, and I admire them for their courage.

No, I have no problem with teachers. What I do have a problem with are the powerful unions that profess to represent teachers' best interests but, instead, act in ways that harm the very enterprise of teaching and learning itself. The NEA and other major teachers' unions, as we have seen throughout this book, have evolved over time into vast empires whose primary goal is to maintain (or expand) their own power and reach, no matter what the cost. They often paint themselves as the champions of children and teachers, but this is deeply dishonest and highly misleading. When the big teachers' unions oppose change because it will upset the status quo—when they try to strangle every effort to better the current system—they are not doing children or even their teachers any favors. Over time, in fact, I believe that the big teachers' unions have taken on an existence that directly counters the best interests of the education system in which they operate. In serving themselves, they are ill serving everybody else: teachers and children, taxpayers, communities, and more.

This is why I have argued throughout this book that the NEA and other belligerent teachers' unions represent the most imposing barrier to authentic school reform that school reformers face today. When I say this in private and public conversations with others who are concerned with figuring out how to improve our nation's schools, someone always retorts that teachers' union activity is not the only stumbling block impeding reform. In fact, I don't disagree with them. Of course there are other barriers to providing excellent schools for all children. But none of these other barriers has a national infrastructure anywhere near as potent as the NEA's. Not one can match its sophisticated communication network, massive budget, organized political support base, or membership rosters that number in the hundreds of thousands. Indeed, no other school reform barrier can generate millions of dollars, or thousands of people, at a moment's notice to rally for or against an issue or a candidate.

The simple fact is that the NEA and other belligerent teacher unions are without par as school reform barriers. School reform initiatives are almost always doomed when the NEA chooses to oppose them, as they usually do. If you want further evidence, reflect on the governor of California's recent attempts to get several school reform initiatives passed in his state.

Why is it so important to lay bare the NEA's role in opposing meaningful and lasting school reform, as I have sought to do in this book? First, notwithstanding the existence of some islands of excellence, the majority of America's schools are not operating at a level of proficiency that meets the current, or future, needs of a great nation. This is an urgent matter of great national importance. Second, even after spending billions of dollars, countless hours of professional and civic effort, and untold amounts of emotional energy and political capital trying to elevate the proficiency of our schools, efforts to improve the productivity of our schools have achieved little to nothing. More than two decades after "A Nation at Risk," we have far too little to show for our efforts.

If we are serious about significantly improving our education system, as opposed to simply fiddling with it, our first imperative must be to correctly identify the factors that now impede school effectiveness. To do so we need a proper diagnosis in order to determine the proper treatment. Why have we achieved so few positive results from so much reform effort in the past? Have we been doing the wrong things? Or have we been doing the right things in the wrong ways? Or some of each?

These questions have many answers, and some are more valid than others. But as I have stated previously, I believe the main problem is this: we have failed to correctly identify and properly address issues of school ineffectiveness associated with the behavior of the NEA and other belligerent teachers' unions.

The educational landscape is littered with the relics of failed educational reform efforts: teacher testing, site-based management, career ladder, curriculum alignment, student testing, team teaching, higher standards, accountability, and computer-assisted instruction, just to name a few. Many of these initiatives added some value, but none of them, individually or collectively, produced the effective school system we need to power America through the first half of the twenty-first century.

Over and over again, we have identified a problem with our schools and sought to fix it. And over and over again, the real solution to our problem has yet to be found. Meanwhile, the power of the big teachers' unions, and their influence over the operations of schools, has not only continued unchecked but in some instances has actually grown stronger. As Walter Cronkite used to say as he ended his daily news program, "and that's the way it is."

But it doesn't have to be that way. Teachers' unions need not be an antireform force. Historically, and up to the present, some teachers' unions and school reformers are working together to create a better education system for the children in their communities and beyond. There have always been, and still are, thoughtful and caring union officials who understand the message that Adam Urbanski, the renowned Rochester, New York, union leader, conveyed when he said to a union audience in 2001: "If the cow dies, there will be no milk for anyone." It doesn't have to be that way because there have been, and still are, union officials who understand the nation's desperate need for school change, and who support such change, instead of warring against it.

Where is the evidence for these bold assertions? There is no better place to begin than with the late Al Shanker. One of the founding fathers of teachers' unionism, Shanker may be among the most influential voices in American education.[2] Consider the following statement about Shanker, made by Richard Kahlenberg:

During the 1980s and 1990s, [Al Shanker] sought to transform teacher unions into a powerful voice for education reform, proposing ideas that were highly unconventional for a union president. In fact, the modern accountability movement, right through to the federal No Child Left Behind Act of 2001, owes much to Shanker's relentless calls for high standards, assessments, and consequences for poor performance. Shanker was also an early proponent of public school choice, charter schools (some even credit him with the idea), rigorous knowledge and skills testing for teachers, and extra pay for *master teachers*.... By openly acknowledging the shortcomings of public schools and embracing innovation, he became a much more credible and effective voice for public education than the NEA or other defenders of the status quo.[3]

Can you imagine a contemporary union leader supporting such bold reform initiatives? Shanker proves that "leadership matters." Some, notably the eminent teachers' union scholar Myron Lieberman, might view Shanker's actual education contribution in somewhat less glowing terms, but we find the difference striking. Clearly, Shanker understood that improved public school operations were good not only for students and community but for teachers as well.

Our educational history contains union leaders who have demonstrated the kind of leadership, which suggests that the current *war against hope* doesn't have to be that way. There exist, even today, union leaders who have exhibited the unique ability to achieve, or at least to strive to achieve, the proper balance between the interests of the public education system and the well-being of the union's members.

I would include Randi Weingarten, president of the United Federation of Teachers (UFT), New York City, in this category. Sure, she gives Joel Klein, New York City's commissioner of education, headaches. But I'll bet that even Klein has no doubt that she understands the need for, and is committed to, school improvement for kids.

Of particular note is Ms. Weingarten's leadership in the unprecedented attempt to open a union-operated charter school in New York City. The NEA is at war with the very idea of charter schools, yet the

United Federation of Teachers Elementary Charter School opened for 150 students in September 2005. To the casual observer, the opening of this school may be of little note. But to me, and I'm sure to school reformers across the nation, the opening of this school represents a major step forward toward the AFT and New York Public School System developing common understandings regarding school operational factors that are critical for school success.

Adam Urbanski, president of the Rochester (New York) Teachers Association and vice president of the American Federation of Teachers (AFT), is another union leader I would include in the category of those demonstrating that it doesn't have to be that way. In 1995, Urbanski, along with another local union leader, convened a group of progressive local teachers' union leaders to form an organization called the Teacher Union Reform Network (TURN). On the first page of its Web site, TURN makes the following statement:

> TURN is a union-led effort to restructure the nation's teachers' unions to promote reforms that will ultimately lead to better learning and higher achievement for America's children.[4]

That's a bold statement. And they go further:

> The TURN Mission Statement recognizes that the past adversarial relationship among union leaders, teachers, and administrators must be replaced with a compact that says "we are all in this together." Everyone recognizes that this will be difficult, but, succeeding in this new and unpredictable environment can only be assured by the mutual effort of administrators, union leaders and teachers, and the creation of a new social framework to hold it together."[5]

Note the phrase: "we are all in this together." Many years ago, Urbanski and I were speaking to a teachers' union audience. I was up first. In an attempt to make the point that we should work together, I used a phrase that Barbara Jordan coined when speaking of our nation's need for the various racial communities to work together. Paraphrasing Barbara, I declared in a loud and proud voice, "We may have come to this country in different ships, but we are in the same boat now. And it's better for all of us if we row together."

Following my remarks, Urbanski took the mike and declared boldly, "If we are all in the same boat together . . . and the boat is leaking . . . then it doesn't matter which end of the boat you are on. We are all going down together."

TURN is unique in that it is one of the few places in the country where union leaders can gather in a safe and collegial environment to discuss progressive union issues. For the most part, TURN's members practice "double bottom line" collective bargaining—that is, they focus both on what is best for the students in their school systems, as well as for what is best for teachers. In its first ten years, TURN has set the stage for conversations about the union's role in advancing student achievement, considering differentiated compensation and other innovative and cutting-edge reforms. Their numbers are small, but their voice has been vitally important in the dialogue about how teachers' unions can become a positive force for change in American public schools.

All across the country, there are isolated examples of teachers' unions and school district officials working together, in contrast to the norm of adversarial warfare. Notable examples can be found in teacher compensation reforms underway or under discussion in Denver, Colorado; Chattanooga, Tennessee; and in school districts in North Carolina and Pennsylvania. These locales have one thing in common: high-quality union leadership.

The union leader I know best is Gayle Fallon, the leader of the Houston Federation of Teachers. During my seven-plus years as Superintendent of the Houston Independent School District, there were few days when Gayle and I were not at war with each other. But there were also days when we stood side-by-side on issues that represented the best interest of Houston's children. Although she was a valiant warrior for her organization, I always knew that she understood our need to change, and that after a few good jabs, we would sit down and work together to get things done.

The sum and substance of this matter is that although presently the teachers' unions are leading a war against hope, *there still is hope.* There is hope because of a handful of teachers' union efforts at teachers' union reform. There is hope because there are teachers' union leaders like the ones mentioned above. So, we must build on this flicker of hope and stoke it into a fire.

The bottom line is this: As a nation, we have a choice between two alternatives. We can choose to have authentic school reform, or we can choose—through omission—to have continued teachers' union dominance of school operations. We cannot have it both ways.

APPENDIX A

MAXIMS OF AMERICAN EDUCATION
(LESSONS FROM LIFE
IN THE PUBLIC ARENA)

Maxim No. 1: Change *is* coming.
Corollary: Americans demand and embrace accountability in nearly every sector of life—from car safety and drug innovations to airline deregulation and cellular competition. It is only a matter of time before the public demands a system that can prove that it serves the needs of children, holds education officials accountable, and rewards the teachers and principals who implement change and curricula that work.

Maxim No. 2: The American people are becoming educated about education.
Corollary: The most important thing for improving public education is to educate the public. The most important thing for educating the public is communicating the enormous magnitude of spending and resources that have already been directed to government-run schools.

Maxim No. 3: The spending argument is spent.
Corollary: Spending is not the only measure of what is going on in the schools. But it is the least important.

Maxim No. 4: The status quo will oppose change. The guardians of mediocrity are the true danger to our public schools. The longer reform is frustrated and the longer failure persists, the more violent the shock to the status quo.

Maxim No. 5: The failure and stagnation of government-run schools directly mirror the growth in power of teachers' unions.
Corollary: The power over schools that is sought by teachers' unions is directly related to the magnitude of the failure of such schools to be able to change and improve.

Observations for Teachers on the Current Behavior of Their Unions

First Observation: Teachers' unions are a special interest. Teachers' unions are a special interest. Teachers' unions are a special interest.

Second Observation: Though teachers' unions are a special interest, that interest is not in the welfare of teachers. If it were, with the money and influence unions have, teachers would be paid better. But they are still underpaid, while a handful of union officials and political causes are the real beneficiaries of teachers' unions.

Third Observation: Teachers' unions advocate as much openness and accountability for our nation's schools to parents as teachers' unions allow openness and accountability about their political actions to their own members—which is zero.

OBSERVATIONS OF UNION TACTICS

Reality Check No. 1 on Unions: Teachers' unions believe children will only learn when we spend enough. Teachers' unions believe that we can never spend enough.

Reality Check No. 2 on Unions: No amount of money can make a broken system work.

Paige's Law of Inevitable and Sustained Blame: Union leaders must never own up to their role in failure. Preferred tactics: Pass the buck; blame the people above you; resist any measures of how children are doing by shifting the burden of change to those above you. Principals blame superintendents, superintendents blame local school boards, local school boards blame state regulations and state superintendents, state superintendents blame state school boards and state lawmakers, state officials blame the federal government . . .

Paige's Iron Law of Success: Every successful school—whether rich or poor, black, white, or Hispanic—succeeds for exactly the same reasons: a singular focus on the belief that every child is expected to learn, implementation of proven curricula in the basics, accountability for progress measured by meaningful testing, and a corps of dedicated and qualified teachers who establish an orderly environment that reinforces respect for learning.

Corollary: Every failing school has a multitude of excuses and its own reasons for why it is failing.

ACKNOWLEDGMENTS

On the cover of this book, a single name appears as the author. However, as most readers and certainly most writers know, rarely does this represent the truth. This work is no exception. I do not wish to go further before I have, to the best of my ability, expressed my deep and abiding appreciation to the many individuals who contributed to this book from start to finish. It is a difficult task because I have learned so much from so many good and caring individuals who, like me, are struggling to make America better by enhancing educational opportunities for all of its children.

I thank those who provided indirect support by helping to deepen both my thinking and my resolve to write this book. These include the authors of books and reports that I have read; seminars and lectures that I have attended; and most of all, wonderful schools that I have visited—schools that, against all odds, are achieving amazing student performance.

I also want to extend my deepest gratitude to those who provided direct assistance in this work by helping sift through mounds of research, sharing their relevant experiences, and providing extremely helpful critiques of successive drafts.

The first among these is Matt Robinson, a great writer and friend whose assistance with the writing constituted only a sliver of his contribution. Mark Hemingway's diligent research helped provide the foundation for this work. Lynn Jenkins, one of the most prolific writers, editors, and education scholars I know, pushed my thinking and sharpened my prose. And my personal assistant, Amy Shah, provided the overall coordination, along with research and writing assistance and the occasional kick in the pants needed to keep the project on course.

I also want to thank Mike Petrilli (Fordham Foundation), Jeanne Allen (Center for Education Reform), Rick Hess (American Enterprise Institute), Brian Jones (College Loan Corporation), and those at the Chartwell Education Group for providing their guidance and critiques to this piece of work. Your insights have been extremely valuable to me.

I also extend my heartfelt appreciation to all who shared their experiences with me and whose stories brought this book to life.

Finally, and perhaps most importantly, I want to express my appreciation and admiration to the countless teachers across the country who, despite adverse pressures from their unions, continue to uphold the highest standards of the teaching profession and do what is right for children.

To all of you, and to the myriad of other individuals and organizations that helped along the way, please accept my deepest thanks.

NOTES

Quote
1. John T. Wenders, "The Extent and Nature of Waste and Rent Dissipation in U.S. Public Education," *Cato Journal*, Vol. 25, No. 2 (Spring/Summer 2005).

Preface
1. Jeanne Allen, Transcript from Milken Family Foundation Teacher Quality Conference: Washington DC (17 May 2006).
2. Charles M. Payne and Mariame Kaba, "So Much Reform, So Little Change: Building-Level Obstacles to Urban School Reform," Northwestern University (February 2001), Vol. 2.
3. William Shakespeare, *Macbeth* (Penguin Group (USA), 2000).
4. Larry Tye, *Rising from the Rails: Pullman Porters and the Making of the Black Middle Class* (New York: Holt, Henry & Company, 2005).
5. Steven D. Levitt and Stephen J. Dubner, *Freakonomics: A Rogue Economist Explores the Hidden Side of Everything* (New York: HarperCollins Publishers, 2005).
6. "National Education Association," www.unionfacts.com.

Chapter 1
1. Alexander Hamilton, James Madison, and John Jay, edited by Clinton Rossiter, *The Federalist Papers* (New York: Penguin Putnam, 1961).
2. Editorial, "Spare the Rod, Mr. Paige," *Hartford Courant* (25 February 2004).
3. Editorial, "Over the Top," *Houston Chronicle* (26 February 2004).
4. Ibid.
5. Associated Press, "Paige Calls Teachers Union 'Terrorist Organization,'" *Chattanooga Times Free Press* (24 February 2004).
6. Pamela Johnson Taverner, "Comment about NEA Was Appalling," *Wichita Eagle* (26 February 2004).
7. Deanna Luchs, "To the Editor: 'Terrorists' Label Extreme," *Daily Record* (6 March 2004).
8. Editorial, "NEA Is Not Al-Qaida," *St. Louis Post-Dispatch* (26 February 2004).
9. Ibid.
10. Michael Graham, "Ask Parents Who the Education Terrorists Are," *Jewish World Review* (25 February 2004).
11. Ibid.
12. Letter in response to Editorial, "Spare the Rod, Mr. Paige," *Hartford Courant* (25 February 2004). Letter was published on 5 March 2004. From Paige's personal files.
13. "Education Reform No Joking Matter," *Virginian-Pilot* (25 February 2004).
14. Rod Paige, "Focus on the Children," *Washington Post* (27 February 2004).
15. Ibid.
16. Ibid.
17. "Testimony of Chairman Alan Greenspan before the Committee on

Education and the Workforce, U.S. House of Representatives," The Federal Reserve Board, 11 March 2004, http://www.federalreserve.gov/boarddocs/testimony/2004/20040311/default.htm (accessed 14 June 2006).

Chapter 2

1. "Statistical Abstract of the United States—Section 4: Education," United States Census Bureau, 4 January 2006, http://www.census.gov/prod/2005pubs/06statab/educ.pdf (accessed 17 October 2006).
2. Richard Wolf, "How Federal Spending Has Climbed Since 2001," *USA Today*, 3 April 2006. "President Bush's FY 2004 Education Budget: Spending More, and Spending It More Wisely: More Money Than Ever for Education; Increases Targeted to No Child Left Behind, Special Education, Higher Education," Committee on Education and the Workforce, US House of Representatives, 3 February 2003.
3. "Federal, State and Local Governments: Public Elementary-Secondary Education Data," United States Census Bureau, 1993-2006, http://www.census.gov/govs/www/school.html (accessed 17 October 2006).
4. "D.C.'s Distinction: $16,344 Per Student, but Only 12% Read Proficiently," *Human Events Online*, 23 March 2006, http://www.humanevents.com/article.php?print=yes&id=13458 (accessed 17 October 2006).
5. US Department of Education, Institute of Education Sciences, National Center for Education Statistics, *The Nation's Report Card: Reading, 2005*, NCES 2006-451, 2006.
6. US Department of Education, Institute of Education Sciences, National Center for Education Statistics, *National Assessment of Educational Progress (NAEP), Long-term Trend Mathematics Assessments, 1978–2004*.
7. US Department of Education, Office of Educational Research and Improvement, National Center for Education Statistics, *Pursuing Excellence: A Study of U.S. Twelfth-Grade Mathematics and Science Achievement in International Context*, NCES 98–049, 1998.
8. The National Commission on Excellence in Education, "A Nation at Risk: The Imperative for Educational Reform," A Report to the Nation and Secretary of Education, United States Department of Education, April 1983, http://www.ed.gov/pubs/NatAtRisk/risk.html (accessed 14 June 2006).
9. Ibid.
10. Joe Williams, *Connecting the Dots: Echo Chamber—The National Education Association's Campaign Against NCLB* (Education Sector), July 2006, www.educationsector.org (accessed 28 July 2006).
11. Ibid.

Chapter 3

1. Samuel L. Blumenfeld, "NEA to Target Republicans in 2004," WorldNetDaily.com, 20 August 2003, http://www.worldnetdaily.com/news/article.asp?ARTICLE_ID=34173 (accessed 20 June 2006).
2. For a breakdown of the NEA's financial empire, see Chapter 8: Education's Gravy Train in Myron Lieberman, *The Teacher Unions: How the NEA and*

AFT Sabotage and Hold Students, Parents, Teachers, and Taxpayers Hostage to Bureaucracy (New York: The Free Press, 1997).

3. Sol Stern, "How Teachers' Unions Handcuff Schools," *City Journal*, Vol. 7, No. 2 (Spring 1997).

4. Samuel L. Blumenfeld, "NEA to Target Republicans in 2004," WorldNetDaily.com, 20 August 2003, http://www.worldnetdaily.com/news/article.asp?ARTICLE_ID=34173 (accessed 20 June 2006).

5. Marsha Richards and Lynn Harsh, "Barrier to Learning: How the National Education Association Prevents Students and Teachers from Achieving Academic and Professional Excellence," The Evergreen Freedom Foundation, July 2004.

6. Mike Antonucci, "The National Everything Association," Education Intelligence Agency, August 2001.

7. "National Education Association Supports Bigger More Expensive Government," National Center for Policy Analysis, originally cited from editorial, "Power, Not Pupils," *Investor's Business Daily*, 6 May 1996, http://www.ncpa.org/pd/unions/unionsb.html (accessed 20 June 2006).

8. This also includes the AFT. However, because of the focus of this book and because they are not as much of a driving force among unions, I have chosen to name them here.

9. "Rankings & Estimates Update: A Report of School Statistics," National Education Association, Fall 2005, http://www.nea.org/edstats/images/05rankings-update.pdf (accessed 20 June 2006).

10. G. Gregory Moo, *Power Grab: How the National Education Association Is Betraying Our Children* (Washington DC: Regnery Publishing, 1999).

11. Charlene K. Haar, *The Politics of the PTA*, Chapter 5: The PTA, the NEA, and Education (New Brunswick, NJ: Transaction Publishers, 2002).

12. Myron Lieberman, *The Teacher Unions: How the NEA and AFT Sabotage Reform and Hold Students, Parents, Teachers and Taxpayers Hostage to Bureaucracy* (New York: The Free Press, 1997).

13. Ibid.

14. Dennis Laurence Cuddy, *NEA: Grab for Power: A Chronology of the National Education Association* (Oklahoma City: Hearthstone Publishing, 2000).

15. President John F. Kennedy, "Executive Order 10988: Employee-Management Cooperation in the Federal Service," 1962, http://www.lib.umich.edu/gov-docs/jfkeo/eo/10988.htm (accessed 10 July 2006).

16. Myron Lieberman, *The Teacher Unions: How the NEA and AFT Sabotage Reform and Hold Students, Parents, Teachers and Taxpayers Hostage to Bureaucracy* (New York: The Free Press, 1997).

17. Ibid.

18. Ibid.

19. Allan M. West, *The National Education Association: The Power Base for Education* (New York: The Free Press, 1980).

20. Myron Lieberman, *The Teacher Unions: How the NEA and AFT Sabotage Reform and Hold Students, Parents, Teachers, and Taxpayers Hostage to Bureaucracy* (New York: The Free Press, 1997).

21. Saul D. Alinsky, *Rules for Radicals: A Pragmatic Primer for Realistic Radicals* (New York: Random House, 1971).

22. Ibid. G. Gregory Moo, *Power Grab: How the National Education Association Is Betraying our Children* (Washington DC: Regnery Publishing Inc., 1999)

23. Charlene K. Haar, *The Politics of the PTA*, Chapter 5: The PTA, the NEA, and Education (New Brunswick, NJ: Transaction Publishers, 2002).

24. Ibid.

25. Dennis Laurence Cuddy, *NEA: Grab for Power: A Chronology of the National Education Association* (Oklahoma City: Hearthstone Publishing, Ltd., 2000).

26. Myron Lieberman, *The Teacher Unions: How the NEA and AFT Sabotage Reform and Hold Students, Parents, Teachers, and Taxpayers Hostage to Bureaucracy* (New York: The Free Press, 1997).

27. Dennis Laurence Cuddy, *NEA: Grab for Power: A Chronology of the National Education Association* (Oklahoma City: Hearthstone Publishing, Ltd., 2000).

28. Ibid.

29. G. Gregory Moo, *Power Grab: How the National Education Association Is Betraying our Children* (Washington DC: Regenery Publishing Inc., 1999).

30. D.T. Stallings, "A Brief History of the U.S. Department of Education, 1979-2002," *Phi Delta Kappan*, Vol. 83, No. 09 (May 2002), p. 677-83. Dennis Laurence Cuddy, *NEA: Grab for Power: A Chronology of the National Education Association* (Oklahoma City: Hearthstone Publishing, Ltd., 2000).

31. "Department of Education," Office of Management and Budget (2005), http://www.whitehouse.gov/omb/budget/fy2005/education.html (accessed 10 July 2006).

32. Dennis Laurence Cuddy, *NEA: Grab for Power: A Chronology of the National Education Association* (Oklahoma City: Hearthstone Publishing, Ltd., 2000).

33. Ibid. The NEA withdrew its lawsuit against Ms. Suzanne Clark on 2 December 1983.

34. *The American School Board Journal* (1983).

35. Terrel H. Bell, *The Thirteenth Man: A Reagan Cabinet Memoir* (New York: The Free Press, 1988).

36. The National Commission on Excellence in Education, "A Nation at Risk: The Imperative for Educational Reform," A Report to the Nation and Secretary of Education, United States Department of Education, April 1983, http://www.ed.gov/pubs/NatAtRisk/risk.html (accessed 14 June 2006).

37. Diane Ravitch, "The Test of Time," *Education Next* (Spring 2003), http://www.educationnext.org/20032/32.html (accessed 10 July 2006). Can also be found, unabridged, as a chapter in: Paul E. Peterson, editor, *Our Schools & Our Future . . . Are We Still at Risk?* Chapter 1: A Historic Document (Stanford, CA: Hoover Press, 2003).

38. Ibid.

39. Transcript, "Reforming School: Riley & Bennett on Education Platforms," *NewsHour with Jim Lehrer*, 23 July 1996, http://www.pbs.org/newshour/bb/education/education_debate_7-23.html (accessed 10 July 2006).

40. "National Education Association Supports Bigger More Expensive

Government," National Center for Policy Analysis, originally cited from: Editorial, "Power, Not Pupils," *Investor's Business Daily*, 6 May 1996, http://www.ncpa.org/pd/unions/unionsb.html (accessed 20 June 2006).

41. Dennis Laurence Cuddy, *NEA: Grab for Power: A Chronology of the National Education Association* (Oklahoma City: Hearthstone Publishing, Ltd., 2000).

Chapter 4

1. Marsha Richards and Lynn Harsh, "Barrier to Learning: How the National Education Association Prevents Students and Teachers from Achieving Academic and Professional Excellence," The Evergreen Freedom Foundation (July 2004).

2. Ibid. Jonathan Schorr, "Hot for Teachers: John Kerry's Quietly Radical School Reform Plan; Politics," *Washington Monthly* (1 July 2004).

3. "NEA Memo: Kerry Backs Away from 'Pay for Performance,'" Education Intelligence Agency, 24 May 2004, http://www.eiaonline.com/archives/20040524.htm (accessed 21 June 2006).

4. "Democratic Leadership Council Blueprint Poll," conducted by Penn Schoen & Barland Associates, 17-20 June 1999, http://www.pollingreport.com/edu2.htm (accessed 21 June 2006).

5. Ibid.

6. Paul E. Peterson, "If Unions Are So Powerful, Why Are Teachers Not Better Paid?" *Government Union Review*, Vol. 20, No. 4 (2003), http://www.psrf.org/gur/gur20.4peterson.jsp (accessed 25 June 2006).

7. Ibid.

8. Ibid.

9. Ibid.

10. Thomas Sowell, *Inside American Education: The Decline, the Deception, the Dogmas* (New York: The Free Press, 1993).

11. Ibid.

12. For more information regarding this, see *Spring Branch Independent School District v. Charles A. Trammell*.

13. Ibid.

14. Esther Kang, "Teachers Union Says Cheating Wrong, but Cites 'Pressure' for High Test Scores," *Medill News Service*, Northwestern University (2 October 2002).

15. Peter F. Drucker, *The Frontiers of Management: Where Tomorrow's Decisions Are Being Shaped Today* (New York: Penguin Putnam Inc., 1999).

16. Paul E. Peterson, "If Unions Are So Powerful, Why Are Teachers Not Better Paid?" *Government Union Review*, Vol. 20, No. 4 (2003), http://www.psrf.org/gur/gur20.4peterson.jsp (accessed 25 June 2006).

17. Sol Stern, "How Teachers' Union Handcuff Schools," Manhattan Institute, *City Journal* (Spring 1997).

18. Peter F. Drucker, *The Frontiers of Management: Where Tomorrow's Decisions Are Being Shaped Today* (New York: Penguin Putnam Inc., 1999).

19. Thomas Sowell, *Inside American Education: The Decline, the Deception, the Dogmas* (New York: The Free Press, 1993).

20. Richard Lee Colvin, "Teachers Who Fail and Keep Teaching; Administrators Blame Tenure's Flaws and Districts' Reluctance to Fire Problem Personnel. But Instructors Also Cite Poor Management. Either Way, the Students Suffer," *Los Angeles Times* (4 June 1995).

21. Thomas Toch, Robin M. Bennefield, Dana Hawkins, and Penny Loeb, "Why Teachers Don't Teach," *U.S. News and World Report*, Vol. 120, No. 8 (26 February 1996).

22. Edwin M. Bridges, *The Incompetent Teacher: The Challenge and the Response* (Washington DC: Falmer Press, 1986).

23. Ibid.

24. Thomas Toch, Robin M. Bennefield, Dana Hawkins, and Penny Loeb, "Why Teachers Don't Teach," *U.S. News and World Report*, Vol. 120, No. 8 (26 February 1996).

25. Edwin M. Bridges, *The Incompetent Teacher: The Challenge and the Response* (Washington DC: Falmer Press, 1986).

26. Thomas Toch, Robin M. Bennefield, Dana Hawkins, and Penny Loeb, "Why Teachers Don't Teach," *U.S. News and World Report*, Vol. 120, No. 8 (26 February 1996).

27. Ibid.

28. La Rae G. Munk, "Collective Bargaining: Bringing Education to the Table: Analysis of 583 Michigan School Labor Contracts and Recommended Improvements to Help Teachers, Schools, and Students" (Midland, MI: Mackinac Center for Public Policy, 1998).

29. Paul E. Peterson, "If Unions Are So Powerful, Why Are Teachers Not Better Paid?" *Government Union Review*, Vol. 20, No. 4 (2003), http://www.psrf.org/gur/gur20.4peterson.jsp (accessed 25 June 2006).

30. Jerry Jesness, "*Stand and Deliver* Revisited," *Reason* (July 2002), http://www.reason.com/0207/fe.jj.stand.shtml (accessed 25 June 2006).

31. Ibid.

32. David W. Kirkpatrick, "Teacher Unions and Educational Reform: The View from Inside," *Government Union Review*, Vol. 19, No. 2, http://www.psrf.org/gur/gur_19.2_kirkpatrick.jsp (accessed 25 June 2006).

33. Jerry Jesness, "*Stand and Deliver* Revisited," *Reason* (July 2002), http://www.reason.com/0207/fe.jj.stand.shtml (accessed 25 June 2006).

34. Ibid.

35. Ibid.

36. Ibid.

37. Ibid.

38. Ibid.

39. Sol Stern, "How Teachers' Union Handcuff Schools," *City Journal* (Spring 1997).

40. Ibid.

Chapter 5

1. Editorial, "Out With the Bad; Reform Storms through the Bunker at LAUSD," *Daily News of Los Angeles* (15 April 1999).

2. Ibid.
3. Rick Orlov and Terri Hardy, "Mayor Calls Los Angeles Board of Education 'Evil and Criminal,'" *Daily News of Los Angeles* (15 September 1998).
4. Ibid.
5. Jim Newton and Doug Smith, "Riordan Task Force Plans Its Own School Board Slate; Education: Group Will Finance Four Candidates to Challenge Incumbents as Mayor Seeks Changes in District," *Los Angeles Times* (12 September 1998).
6. Ibid.
7. Editorial, "Erasing Failure; Mayor Riordan Has a Plan to Replace Silly Board Members with Serious People," *Daily News of Los Angeles* (15 September 1998).
8. Rick Orlov and Terri Hardy, "Mayor Calls Los Angeles Board of Education 'Evil and Criminal,'" *Daily News of Los Angeles* (15 September 1998).
9. Editorial, "Los Angeles Times Interview: School Board Candidates," *Los Angeles Times* (14 March 1999).
10. David R. Baker, "Cortines Gives Details of Subdividing LAUSD," *Daily News of Los Angeles* (12 January 2000).
11. "Los Angeles School Board Files Suit Against Own Lawyers over Belmont Learning Complex," Associated Press, AM cycle (16 September 1999).
12. Editorial, "Shootout at the L.A. Corral," *Los Angeles Times* (8 March 1998).
13. Ibid.
14. Terry Moe, "The Union Label on the Ballot Box," *Education Next*, Summer 2006, http://media.hoover.org/documents/ednext20063_58.pdf (accessed 17 October 2006).
15. Editorial, "We're Ok; You're Not; Los Angeles Doesn't Need Its School Board to Attend Group Therapy Sessions; It Needs a New Group," *Daily News of Los Angeles* (27 January 1999).
16. Ibid.
17. Editorial, "Irresponsible Outrage Meter: 10," *Daily News of Los Angeles* (19 February 1999).
18. Editorial, "Los Angeles Times Interview: School Board Candidates," *Los Angeles Times* (14 March 1999).
19. US Department of Education, Institute for Educational Sciences and the National Center for Educational Statistics, "National Assessment of Educational Progress—Trial Urban District Assessment: Los Angeles, CA" (2005).
20. Editorial, "Los Angeles Times Interview: School Board Candidates," *Los Angeles Times* (14 March 1999).
21. US Department of Education, Institute for Educational Sciences and the National Center for Educational Statistics, "National Assessment of Educational Progress—Trial Urban District Assessment: Los Angeles, CA" (2005).
22. Editorial, "Los Angeles Times Interview: School Board Candidates," *Los Angeles Times* (14 March 1999).

23. Louis Sahagun, "Few Hold Positive View of L.A. School Board; About One-Quarter of Voters Surveyed Support Trustees. Riordan's Endorsements May Sway Key Group in Election," *Los Angeles Times* (4 April 1999).

24. Ibid. These numbers—and numbers like them all over the nation—are reminders that the real threat to traditionally run schools is not advocates of choice. The real threat to the ideal of public schooling is an establishment that fails to reform the schools for the sake of children and to the satisfaction of parents. Continuing failure—not parental choice advocates—is the real threat to the current system.

25. Ibid.

26. Editorial, "Los Angeles Times Interview: School Board Candidates," *Los Angeles Times* (14 March 1999).

27. George Archibald, "Public Schools No Place for Teachers' Kids," *Washington Times* (22 September 2004).

28. Editorial, "Los Angeles Times Interview: School Board Candidates," *Los Angeles Times* (14 March 1999).

29. Ibid.

30. Ibid.

31. Ibid. Some teachers in school districts, especially those that are larger and more urban, are forced to hire emergency credentialed teachers in order to fulfill their minimum teacher quota. These teachers are individuals who are: credentialed teachers teaching out of their subject area; uncredentialed teachers who meet the minimum emergency permit requirements of a bachelor's degree and passage of the state's test of standard, basic skills; or uncredentialed individuals who have some or all of their emergency permit requirements waived. Some of the reasons that this process occurs are: increased student enrollment; increased teacher demands; unavailability and/or inconvenient scheduling of classes needed to finish full teacher credentialing; inadequate teaching conditions; shortages of teachers in key academic disciplines.

32. Editorial, "Four for School Reform; Voting to Make a Change on the LAUSD Board Will Help Fix Education," *Daily News of Los Angeles* (21 March 1999).

33. Editorial, "4 for the School Board," *Los Angeles Times* (21 March 1999).

34. Editorial, "Quit Meddling; That's the Message a Group of L.A.'s Most Successful and Wisest Civic Leaders are Sending to the Board of Education, and We Couldn't Agree More," *Daily News of Los Angeles* (18 February 1999).

35. Editorial, "New Era at School Board," *Los Angeles Times* (15 April 1999).

36. Jill Stewart, "LAUSD Reform on the Line," *Daily News of Los Angeles* (27 February 2003).

37. Ibid.

38. Helen Gao, "Unions Retake LAUSD; Reformers Young, Hayes Losing to UTLA Candidates," *Daily News of Los Angeles* (5 March 2003).

39. "Legislative Update," *Capitol News of California State University, Northridge,*

7 March 2003, http://www.csun.edu/~govrel/ArchivesJan-June03.html (accessed 17 October 2006).

40. Howard Blume, "A Capricious Fate," *LA Weekly*, 7 March 2003.

41. Howard Blume, "The Reformers Are Dead, Long Live the Reformers," *LA Weekly* (14 March 2003).

42. Ibid.

43. "Bob Hertzberg to Seek Breakup of Los Angeles Unified School District," Press Releases on Bob Hertzberg's changeLA.com, 1 December 2004, http://www.changela.com/docs/04-12-01-PR-LAUSD_BREAKUP_PUBLIC.pdf (accessed 31 July 2006).

44. Howard Blume, "The Reformers Are Dead, Long Live the Reformers," *LA Weekly* (14 March 2003).

45. Joe Williams, "The Labor Management Showdown," in Frederick M. Hess, editor, *Urban School Reform: Lessons from San Diego* (Cambridge, MA: Harvard Education Press, 2005).

46. Julian R. Betts, Andrew C. Zau, and Kevin King, *From Blueprint to Reality: San Diego's Education Reforms* (San Francisco: Public Policy Institute of California, 2005).

47. Larry Cuban and Michael Usdan, "Fast and Top-Down: Systemic Reform and Student Achievement in San Diego City Schools," *Powerful Reforms and Shallow Roots,* (New York: Teachers College Press, 2003).

48. Joe Williams, "The Labor Management Showdown," in Frederick M. Hess, editor, *Urban School Reform: Lessons from San Diego* (Cambridge, MA: Harvard Education Press, 2005).

49. Yvette tenBerge, "Teacher Fired After Making Headlines," *La Prensa San Diego*, 7 June 2002, http://www.laprensa-sandeigo.org/archieve/june07-02/fired.htm (accessed 31 July 2006).

50. Joe Williams, "The Labor Management Showdown," in Frederick M. Hess, editor, *Urban School Reform: Lessons from San Diego* (Cambridge, MA: Harvard Education Press, 2005).

51. Pamela A. Riley, Rosemarie Fusano, La Rae Munk, and Ruben Peterson, "Contract for Failure: The Impact of Teacher Union Contracts on the Quality of California Schools," Pacific Research Institute for Public Policy (March 2002).

52. Helen Raham, "Reinventing Teacher Contracts," Society for the Advancement of Excellence in Education, Fall 2000, http://www.saee.ca/policy/D_010_DDB_LON.php (accessed on 26 June 2006).

53. All comments from Jan LaChapelle come from a personal interview conducted by Mark Hemingway on 1 September 2004.

54. Pamela A. Riley, Rosemarie Fusano, Larae Munk, and Ruben Peterson, "Contract for Failure: The Impact of Teacher Union Contracts on the Quality of California School," Pacific Research Institute for Public Policy (March 2002).

55. "Three-fourths of State's Teacher Contracts Remain Unsettled," Education Minnesota, 15 January 2004, http://www.educationminnesota.org/index.cfm?PAGE_ID=9612 (accessed 26 June 2006).

56. This section on the Buffalo public school system draws extensively from a case study: Frederick M. Hess, "The Perfect Storm: School Reform in Buffalo," The Broad Foundation and Center for Reform of School Systems, 2005.

57. Ibid.

58. Ibid.

59. Ibid.

60. Darryl Campagna, "Teachers Strike; City Schools Close as Union Defies Court Order," *Buffalo News*, 7 September 2000.

61. Peter Simon and Darryl Campagna, "School Close as Teachers Renew Strike; Judge Orders BTF Leaders into Court," *Buffalo News*, 14 September 2000.

Chapter 6

1. Stephanie Desmon, "D.C. Teachers Group Seized Under Allegations of Misuse of Dues; Union's Parent Takes Over; Suit Filed Against Officers," *Baltimore Sun*, 1 March 2003.

2. Ibid.

3. Justin Blum, "Audit Says Union Lost $5 Million to Theft; Teachers Group Sues Eight From D.C. Local," *Washington Post*, 17 January 2003.

4. "Statistical Tables—Public Elementary-Secondary Education Finances: 1995-96," United States Census Bureau, 1996, http://ftp2.census.gov/govs/school/96tables.pdf (accessed 17 October 2006).

5. Valerie Strauss and Justin Blum, "Apathy and Secrecy Filled Teachers Union, Many Say," *Washington Post*, 12 January 2003.

6. Ibid

7. Ibid.

8. Joe Mozingo, "Teachers' Group Moves to Tighten Financial Controls," *Miami Herald*, 4 June 2003.

9. Matthew I. Pinzur, "Audit: Union Cheated of $3.5 Million," *Miami Herald*, 5 September 2003.

10. Larry Lebowitz and Joe Mozingo, "Plea in Teachers-Union Corruption Questioned as Being Too Lenient," *Miami Herald*, 31 August 2003.

11. Ibid. Joe Mozingo and Larry Lebowitz, "Tornillo Close to a Deal, Could Go to Jail"

12. Matthew I. Pinzur, "Audit Did Not Report on Tornillo's Spending of Union Money," *Miami Herald*, 17 August 2003.

13. Michael Putney, "Another Official Succumbs to the Arrogance of Power," *Miami Herald*, 27 August 2003; Matthew I. Pinzur, "Audit: Union Cheated of $3.5 Million," *Miami Herald*, 5 September 2003.

14. The UTD, in order to compensate for some of the debt incurred due to these scandals, had to sell their local headquarters. The cost: $22 million. Matthew I. Pinzur, "Teachers Union Sells Headquarters to Get out of Debt," *Miami Herald*, 5 June 2004; Tia Chapman, "Teachers' Union Gets New Home," *Miami Herald*, 18 November 2001.

15. Maya Bell, "Probe Casts Shadow on Educator's Legacy; The Union Leader at

the Center of an FBI Investigation has a Distinguished History," *Orlando Sentinel* (19 May 2003).

16. *Abood v. Detroit Board of Education*, 431 U.S. 209 (1977). Dissenting employees have a constitutional right under the First Amendment to prevent their labor union from using a share of their service fees for certain political and ideological activities unrelated to the union's collective-bargaining activities. Thus, through deception, union leaders regularly divert money they receive from their membership to pay for their partisan agenda.

17. Les Kjos, "Teacher Unions Remain Stable," *United Press International* (10 June 2003).

18. Debbie Cenziper, "A Teacher Feels the Sting of Betrayal," *Miami Herald* (29 September 2003).

19. Ibid.

20. Michael Putney, "Another Official Succumbs to the Arrogance of Power," *Miami Herald* (27 August 2003).

21. Matthew I. Pinzur, "Audit: Union Cheated of $3.5 Million," *Miami Herald* (5 September 2003).

22. Matthew I. Pinzur, "Leaders of UTD Saw Crisis, Kept Silent," *Miami Herald* (17 August 2003).

23. Valerie Strauss and Justin Blum, "Apathy and Secrecy Filled Teachers Union, Many Say," *Washington Post* (12 January 2003).

24. Maya Bell, "Probe Casts Shadow on Educator's Legacy; The Union Leader at the Center of an FBI Investigation has a Distinguished History," *Orlando Sentinel* (19 May 2003).

25. National Labor Relations Act, 29 U.S.C. 151, 158. Section 8(a)(3) permits an employer and a union to enter into an agreement requiring all employees in the bargaining unit to pay union dues as a condition of continued employment, regardless of whether the employees become union members.

26. Stefan Gleason, "No Choice," *National Review Online* (10 February 2003).

27. Ibid.

28. Ibid.

29. Larry Margasak and John Solomon, "NEA's Political Activities Detailed," *Associated Press* (22 June 2000).

30. The NEA is a 501(c)(5) organization. According to 26 U.S.C. Sec. 501, such organizations must report "direct and indirect" political expenses on their tax return. Also see Kate O'Beirne, "Called to the Principal's Office: Judgment Day for the NEA," *National Review* (3 December 2003).

31. Ibid.

32. Glenn Burkins, "Teachers' Unions Will Show Clout as Democrats Meet," *Wall Street Journal* (23 August 1996).

33. Larry Margasak and John Solomon, "NEA's Political Activities Detailed," *Associated Press* (22 June 2000).

34. "Nondeductible Lobbying and Political Expenditures," Internal Revenue Service, United States Department of the Treasury, http://www.irs.gov/charities/nonprofits/article/0,id=156145,00.html (accessed 26 June 2006).

35. Editorial, "IRS Auditors Visit the NEA—Finally," *Washington Times* (7 December 2003).
36. Myron Lieberman, *The Teacher Unions: How the NEA and AFT Sabotage Reform and Hold Students, Parents, Teachers, and Taxpayers Hostage to Bureaucracy* (New York: The Free Press, 1997).
37. Geoff Metcalf, "Landmark Legal vs. NEA: Geoff Metcalf Interviews Constitution Defender Mark Levin on Pending Battle," http://www.geoffmetcalf.com/qa/24115.html (accessed 26 June 2006).
38. National Education Association, "About NEA: What We Do," http://www.nea.org/aboutnea/whatwedo.html (accessed 26 June 2006).
39. Mark R. Levin and Richard P. Hutchinson, "2000 IRS Complaint v. NEA," Landmark Legal Foundation.
40. Ibid.
41. Ibid.
42. Ibid.
43. Ibid.
44. Ibid.
45. Ibid.
46. Ibid.
47. Ibid.
48. Ibid.
49. Ibid.
50. Ibid.
51. Ibid.
52. Ibid.
53. "An Institution at Risk: An External Communications Review of the National Education Association," The Kamber Group (14 January 1997).
54. Ibid.
55. Ibid.
56. Ibid.
57. Ibid.
58. Ibid.
59. Geoff Metcalf, "Landmark Legal vs. NEA: Geoff Metcalf Interviews Constitution Defender Mark Levin on Pending Battle," http://www.geoffmetcalf.com/qa/24115.html (accessed 26 June 2006).
60. William McGurn, "Teacher's Pets: Secret Documents Show that the National Education Association Has *Become* the Democratic Party," *Wall Street Journal* (2 August 2001).
61. David Wagner, "Have IRS Audits Become Political?" *Insight on the News* (7 April 1997).
62. Ibid.
63. "Statement of Cameron Findlay, Deputy Secretary, U.S. Department of Labor," Subcommittee on Employer-Employee Relations, Subcommittee on Workforce Protections, Committee on Education and the Workforce, US House of Representatives, 10 April 2002, http://www.house.gov/ed_workforce/hearings/107th/wp/lmrda41002/findlay.htm (accessed 26 June 2006).

64. Bernadette Malone, "The Zeal Against Jeb: For Florida Democrats, It's Payback Time," *National Review*, 11 November 2002.

65. It should be noted that the FEA now claims that they did not in fact take out a mortgage to finance McBride's campaign. They offer up a thoroughly confusing, and almost intentionally obfuscating, explanation for some of their real estate transactions at that time; Bernadette Malone in writing for *National Review* asserts that she initially asked FEA president Maureen Dinnen point blank about the mortgage and that she had confirmed the mortgage story. The FEA immediately began backpedaling as soon as the story appeared in print. Frankly, Malone's story seems far more believable, and this still does in any way detract from the suggestion that the union wasted their money on a partisan vendetta rather than the professional betterment of Florida teachers."Letters," *National Review*, 25 November 2002; Bernadette Malone, "The Zeal Against Jeb: For Florida Democrats, It's Payback Time," *National Review*, 11 November 2002.

66. Lloyd Dunkelberger and Gary Fineout, "Conflict Further Ties Up McBride Election Case," *The Ledger* (Lakeland, FL), 1 February 2004.

67. John B. Judis, "Lose-Lose," *New Republic*, 24 January 2000.

68. "NEA Memo: Kerry Backs Away from 'Pay for Performance,'" Education Intelligence Agency, 24 May 2004, http://www.eiaonline.com/archives/20040524.htm (accessed 31 July 2006).

69. Associated Press, "IRS auditing National Education Association," cnn.com, 25 November 2003, http://www.cnn.com/2003/EDUCATION/11/25/teachers.irs.ap/index.html. Also see Larry Margasak, "IRS Audits Nation's Top Teachers' Union," Landmark Legal Foundation, 24 November 2003.

70. George Archibald, "NEA Spends More than $1 Million to Back Kerry," *Washington Times*, 29 October 2004.

71. Megan McArdle, "Make Up Your Mind Already!!!" Instapundit.com, 29 October 2004, http://instapundit.com/archives/018751.php (accessed 26 June 2006).

72. This search was last conducted on the Google Web site on 26 June 2006.

73. Jill Stewart, "CTA Could Be Big Loser in Fight Over Dues," *Los Angeles Daily News*, 30 October 2005.

74. Mark Martin, "The Special Election: Looking Ahead; Unions: Labor Was United Against Initiatives of Governor, but Can the Togetherness Last?," *San Francisco Chronicle*, 10 November 2005.

75. For a detailed breakdown of presidential expenditures see "2004 Presidential Election," Opensecrets.org, http://www.opensecrets.org/presidential/index.asp?sort=R (accessed 26 June 2006).

76. Mark Martin, "The Special Election: Looking Ahead; Unions: Labor Was United Against Initiatives of Governor, but Can the Togetherness Last?" *San Francisco Chronicle*, 10 November 2005.

77. Jill Stewart, "Public Unions Become State's New Barons," *Daily News of Los Angeles*, 16 October 2005.

78. Ibid.

79. Judy Liegmann, "Teachers Union Doesn't Speak for All Teachers," *San Jose Mercury News*, 26 October 2005.

80. The California Voter Foundation, www.calvoter.org.

81. Jill Stewart, "Public Unions Become State's New Barons," *Daily News of Los Angeles*, 16 October 2005.

82. "Action on NBIs and Other Business," *Education Intelligence Agency*, 6 July 2005, http://www.eiaonline.com/archives/20050706.htm (accessed 26 June 2006).

Chapter 7

1. Richard D. Kahlenberg, "Philosopher or King?" *Education Next*, 14 January 2003, http://www.educationnext.org/20033/34.html (accessed 21 June 2006).

2. F. Howard Nelson, Bella Rosenberg, and Nancy Van Meter, "Charter School Achievement on the 2003 National Assessment of Educational Progress," *American Federation of Teachers, AFL-CIO*, August 2004.

3. Diana Jean Schemo, "Charter Schools Trail in Results, U.S. Data Reveals," *New York Times*, 17 August 2004.

4. Rod Paige, "Paige Issues Statement Regarding, *New York Times* Article on Charter Schools," US Department of Education, 17 August 2004, http://www.ed.gov/news/pressreleases/2004/08/08172004.html (accessed 21 June 2006).

5. Ibid.

6. F. Howard Nelson, Bella Rosenberg, and Nancy Van Meter, "Charter School Achievement on the 2003 National Assessment of Educational Progress," *American Federation of Teachers, AFL-CIO*, August 2004.

7. US Department of Education. Institute of Education Sciences, National Center for Education Statistics, *America's Charter Schools: Results from the NAEP 2003 Pilot Study*, NCES 2005-456, National Center for Education Statistics (Washington DC: 2004).

8. F. Howard Nelson, Bella Rosenberg, and Nancy Van Meter, "Charter School Achievement on the 2003 National Assessment of Educational Progress," *American Federation of Teachers, AFL-CIO*, August 2004.

9. William G. Howell, Paul E. Peterson, and Martin R. West, "Dog Eats AFT Homework," *Wall Street Journal*, 18 August 2004.

10. Mickey Kaus, "*Kf*'s Long-Overdue Push-Back!" 20 August 2004, http://slate.msn.com/id/2105245 (accessed 21 June 2006).

11. Matthew Yglesias, "Lagging Charters," http://www.prospect.org/archives/archives/2004/08/index.html (accessed 21 June 2006).

12. "Live By the Sword, Die By *The Times*," Eduwonk.com, 15 August 2004, http://eduwonk.com/archives/2004_08_15_archive.html (accessed 21 June 2006).

13. Diana Jean Schemo, "Charter Schools Trail in Results, U.S. Data Reveals," *New York Times* (17 August 2004).

14. "Charter Schools Produce Strong Student Achievement," The Center for Education Reform, 17 August 2004, http://www.edreform.com/index.cfm?fuseAction=document&documentID=1806 (accessed 21 June 2006).

15. Diana Jean Schemo, "Charter Schools Trail in Results, U.S. Data Reveals," *New York Times* (17 August 2004).
16. Steve Patterson and Rosalind Rossi, "Daley Defends Charter Schools Here as a Success," *Chicago Sun-Times* (19 August 2004).
17. Ibid.
18. Ibid.
19. "National Charter School Clearinghouse Newsletter—Myth of the Month," National Charter School Clearinghouse (February 2002), Vol. 1, No. 2, https://www.ncsc.info/newsletter/February_2002/myth.htm (accessed 21 June 2006).
20. Ibid.
21. Ofelia Madrid, "NE Valley Charter Schools Rank Among the Best in Stanford 9 Scores," *Arizona Republic* (21 August 2004).
22. Marjorie Coeyman, "Charter Schools Build on a Decade of Experimentation," *Christian Science Monitor* (7 January 2003).
23. "LAYC—The Next Step Public Charter School," The Next Step, http://www.layc-dc.org/charterschools/nextstep.html (accessed 21 June 2006).
24. "Charter Schools: Fact and Fiction," *New York Post* (20 November 2004).
25. "Charter Schools Produce Strong Student Achievement," The Center for Education Reform, 17 August 2004, http://www.edreform.com/index.cfm?fuseAction=document&documentID=1806 (accessed 21 June 2006).
26. Lewis C. Solomon and Pete Goldschmidt, "Policy Report: Comparison of Traditional Public Schools and Charter Schools on Retention, School Switching, and Achievement Growth," The Goldwater Institute (15 March 2004), No. 192.
27. John F. Whitte, David L. Weimer, Paul A. Schlomer, and Arnold F. Shober, "The Performance of Charter Schools in Wisconsin," The Robert La Follette School of Public Affairs, University of Wisconsin-Madison (August 2004).
28. Daniel L. Quisenberry, "Highlights from Charter MEAP Data 2003," Michigan Association of Public School Academies (2003).
29. "Charter Schools Produce Strong Student Achievement," The Center for Education Reform, 17 August 2004, http://www.edreform.com/index.cfm?fuseAction=document&documentID=1806 (accessed 21 June 2006).
30. Sam Dillon, "Washington Votes Down New Format for Schools," *New York Times* (4 November 2004).
31. Geov Parrish, "Political Education," *Seattle Weekly* (6 September 2000).
32. "Drop Union Opposition to Charter Schools in Detroit," *Detroit News* (20 July 2004).
33. Ibid.
34. George A. Clowes, "Charter School Growth Slows as Opposition Intensifies: Fighting in the 'War Against Charter Schools,'" Heartland Institute (1 December 2002).
35. Stefan Gleason, "How the NEA Thwarts Education Reform," National Right to Work Legal Defense Foundation, Inc., 23 January 1999, www.nrtw.org/b/SHGcnp.htm (accessed 21 June 2006).

36. George A. Clowes, "Charter School Growth Slows as Opposition Intensifies: Fighting in the 'War Against Charter Schools,'" Heartland Institute (1 December 2002).

37. "Fact Sheet: Nashville-Davidson (balance), Tennessee: 2004 American Community Survey Data Profile Highlights," American FactFinder, US Census Bureau, 2004, http://factfinder.census.gov/servlet/ACSSAFFFacts?_event=&geo_id=16000US4752006&_geoContext=01000US%7C04000US47%7C16000US4752006&_street=&_county=nashville%2C+tn&_cityTown=nashville%2C+tn&_state=&_zip=&_lang=en&_sse=on&ActiveGeoDiv=&_useEV=&pctxt=fph&pgsl=160&_submenuId=factsheet_0&ds_name=DEC_2000_SAFF&_ci_nbr=null&qr_name=null&reg=null%3Anull&_keyword=&_industry= (accessed 21 June 2006).

38. Claudette Riley, "New KIPP Charter School Won't Open This Fall," *Tennessean* (21 May 2004).

39. Daniel Weintraub, "Teacher Union Fights to Hold Sacramento High Down," *Sacramento Bee* (3 July 2003).

40. Ibid.

41. Ibid.

42. David W. Kirkpatrick, "Teacher Unions Continue Attack on Charter Schools," The Buckeye Institute for Public Policy Solutions, 4 July 2004, http://www.buckeyeinstitute.org/article/83 (accessed 21 June 2006).

43. Terry Ryan, "A Wide-Angle Look at the Charter School Movement in Ohio/Dayton, Circa September 2004," The Thomas B. Fordham Foundation and The KIDS School Resource Center (September 2004).

44. Ibid.

45. Ibid.

46. Catherine Candinsky, "Charters Face Supreme Test," *Columbus Dispatch* (26 November 2005).

47. Terry Ryan, "A Wide-Angle Look at the Charter School Movement in Ohio/Dayton, Circa September 2004," The Thomas B. Fordham Foundation and The KIDS School Resource Center (September 2004).

48. Ibid.

49. Ibid.

50. Kelley O. Beaucar, "Union Targets Charter Schools," Foxnews.com, 11 July 2001, http://www.foxnews.com/story/0,2933,29241,00.html (accessed 21 June 2006).

51. David W. Kirkpatrick, "Many Teachers Favor Charter Schools Although Their Unions Don't," The Buckeye Institute for Public Policy Scholars, 20 May 2004, http://www.buckeyeinstitute.org/article/88 (accessed 21 June 2006).

52. David W. Kirkpatrick, "Teacher Unions Continue Attack on Charter Schools," The Buckeye Institute for Public Policy Solutions, 4 July 2004, http://www.buckeyeinstitute.org/Articles/2004_052.htm (accessed 21 June 2006).

53. Ibid.

54. Ibid.

55. "Live By the Sword, Die By *The Times*," Eduwonk.com, 15 August 2004, http://eduwonk.com/archives/2004_08_15_archive.html (accessed 21 June 2006).

Chapter 8

1. Richard Wolf, "How Federal Spending has Climbed Since 2001," *USA Today* (3 April 2006). "President Bush's FY 2004 Education Budget: Spending More, and Spending It More Wisely: More Money Than Ever for Education; Increases Targeted to No Child Left Behind, Special Education, Higher Education," Committee on Education and the Workforce, US House of Representatives (3 February 2003).
2. As quoted in "A Breakthrough on Education Reform," *New Dem Daily [Democratic Leadership Council]* (12 December 2001).
3. "Letter from House and Senate New Democrats to President Bush on Education Reform," 26 February 2001, http://www.dlc.org/ndol_ci.cfm?kaid=110&subid=134&contentid=3083 (accessed 26 June 2006).
4. Howard Good, "Losing It: The Confessions of an Ex-School Board President," *Education Week* (17 March 2004).
5. David W. Kirkpatrick, "Dissatisfaction with Public Schools Evident," Oklahoma Council of Public Affairs, 3 September 2004, http://www.ocpathink.org/ViewEvent.asp?ID=91 (accessed 26 June 2006).
6. Ibid.
7. Editorial, "Erasing Failure; Mayor Riordan Has a Plan to Replace Silly Board Members with Serious People," *Daily News of Los Angeles* (15 September 1998).
8. Jean Johnson and John Immerwahr, "First Things First: What Americans Expect from the Public Schools," Public Agenda (5 October 1994).
9. Jean Johnson and Steve Farkas, "Getting By: What American Teenagers Really Think about Their Schools," Public Agenda (11 February 1997).
10. "'Getting By': Public School Students Want Higher Standards," *Daily Report Card* (12 February 1997).
11. Meredith May, "A Program Trying to Turn At-Risk Youth into Scholars; KIPP Kids Attend from 7:30 a.m. to 5 p.m., Wear Uniforms, Must Walk in Single-File Lines," *San Francisco Chronicle* (29 December 2003).
12. "Major Achievements for Local Charter School," ABC7, 23 September 2004, http://www.kippbayview.org/news_events_ABC7_2004.htm (accessed 19 June 2006).
13. Ibid.
14. Ibid.
15. Ibid.
16. "Childs Elementary School," Greatschools.net, 2004–2005, http://www.greatschools.net/cgi-bin/il/other/3407 (accessed 19 June 2006).
17. Crystal Yednak and Darnell Little, "Scores Reveal Surprise Gap" and "Overshadowed School Shines on State Tests," *Chicago Tribune* (13 November 2002).
18. Ibid.

19. Ibid.
20. Edward Moscovitch, "School's Success Is One of a Kind," *Boston Herald* (6 October 2002).
21. Ibid.
22. Ibid.
23. Patte Barth, Kati Haycock, Hilda Jackson, Karen Mora, Pablo Ruiz, Stephanie Robinson, and Amy Wilkins, "Dispelling the Myth: High Poverty Schools Exceeding Expectations," Education Trust and Council of Chief State School Officers (1999).
24. Ibid.
25. Lance Izumi, K. Gwynne Coburn, and Matt Cox, "They Have Overcome: High-Poverty, High Performance Schools in California," Pacific Research Institute (September 2002).
26. Ibid.
27. Ibid.
28. "Secretary of Education Rod Paige on Faith and Schools," *Baptist Press*, 12 May 2003, http://findarticles.com/p/articles/mi_qa3827/is_200305/ ai_n9264426 (accessed 19 June 2006).
29. David Finley, "Legislation Won't Make Children Learn," *Arizona Republic*, 10 December 2002, http://www.tuff-teach.com/pcs//showthread.php?t=2932 (accessed 19 June 2006).
30. Ibid.
31. "Achievement Matters: A Mesa Public Schools Newsletter for Parents," Webster Elementary School (October 2002).
32. "Lincoln Elementary School," Greatschools.net, 2004–2005, http:www.greatschools.net/cgi-bin/az/other/913 (accessed 19 June 2006).
33. "Lincoln Elementary School," Greatschools.net, 2004–2005, http:www.great schools.net/modperl/achievement/az/913 (accessed 19 June 2006).

Chapter 9

1. Peter F. Drucker, *Post-Capitalist Society* (New York: HarperCollins Publishers, Inc., 1993).
2. Richard Florida, *The Flight of the Creative Class: The New Global Competition for Talent* (New York: HarperCollins Publishers, Inc., 2005).
3. Terry Atlas, "Bangalore's Big Dreams," *U.S. News & World Report*, 2 May 2005, http://www.usnews.com/usnews/biztech/articles/050502/2india.htm (accessed 21 June 2006).
4. Josh Douglas, Eric Iverson and Chitra Kalyandurg, "Engineering in the K-12 Classroom: An Analysis of Current Practices and Guidelines for the Future," The American Society for Engineering Education (November 2004).
5. Doug Lederman, "Accessing College 'Access and Accountability,'" *Insider Higher Education*, 29 April 2005, http://insidehighered.com/news/2005/04/29/hea (accessed 21 June 2006).
6. Sandra Feldman, "When a School Fails," September 1997, http://www.aft.org/presscenter/speeches-columns/wws/1997/0997.htm (accessed 21 June 2006).

7. "The Nation's Report Card: Mathematics 2003," National Center for Education Statistics, US Department of Education, Institute of Education Sciences (Washington DC: US Government Printing Office, 2005). "The Nation's Report Card: Reading 2003," National Center for Education Statistics, US Department of Education, Institute of Education Sciences (Washington DC: US Government Printing Office, 2005).
8. "No Lessons Left Behind," *USA Today* (20 July 2005).
9. "Turning the Page; Our Stand: Increases in Reading Skills Are Welcome News," *Arizona Republic* (5 August 2005).
10. William L. Taylor, "Op-Ed: Good News in Public Education," 25 July 2005, www.civilrights.org (accessed 21 June 2006).
11. "A Bullish Report on Public Schools," *Virginian-Pilot* (25 July 2005).

Chapter 10

1. Albert Shanker, "The End of Our Traditional Model of Schooling—and a Proposal for Using Incentives to Restructure Our Public Schools," Phi Delta Kappan (January 1990).
2. Richard D. Kahlenberg, "Philosopher or King?" *Education Next*, Spring 2003.
3. Ibid.
4. Teacher Union Reform network. Main homepage: http://gseis.ucla.edu/ hosted/turn/turn.html.
5. Ibid.

INDEX